INSPIRED|MOMENTS

Little did I know, in our mutually dark time, you would find a way to pull strength out of me I didn't know I had. Though you needed help, you sacrificed your needs and helped me. I wondered how you managed to give when you were empty. Your response was "give to God off the top and he'll make sure you're never without and pull you thru". God did that; for both of us and I will be forever grateful to you. You're my greatest inspiration; always has been and always will be.

    — INSPIRED|L.Wiggins

Our chats about "small acts of kindness" and how they can drastically change someone's life have been the GREATEST inspiration. I recognized and confirmed my belief that all it takes is for one person to start - and then there is a movement. And here you are...! #kindness #theGREATrevolution #InspiredLegacy #bytnicole

    — INSPIRED|C.Thompson

For over 12 years, I've known you to make lemonade out of lemons and slay giants that have come your way. From every divine conversation to what I've witnessed with your children, your household and your leadership with your work teams – I am instantly INSPIRED to do more and be more.

In unison, "Without a vision, we will perish, but with a vision we will FLOURISH!" Such truth we have both discovered; and I thank you for the inspiration and fuel to run on a little longer.

    — INSPIRED|G.Carter

INSPIRED|LEGACY

Cultivating Generational Greatness
One Seed at a Time

by T. Nicole

INSPIRED|LEGACY
Cultivating Generational Greatness One Seed at a Time
by T. Nicole

© 2018 by T. Nicole. All rights reserved.

No part of this book may be reproduced in any written, electronic, recording, or photocopying form without written permission of the author, T. Nicole.

Books may be purchased in quantity by contacting the publisher, bTN Publishing and Media Group, at 990 Peachtree Industrial Blvd, Suite 4482, Suwanee, GA 30024; 510-686-4286 or by email at info@bytnicole.com.

Published by: bTN Publishing and Media Group, Atlanta, Georgia

Designed by: bTN Publishing and Media Group, Atlanta, Georgia

Editing by: Divinely Inspired

Creative Consultant: Divinely Inspired

ISBN: 978-0-692-10441-5

Printed in USA

INSPIRED|**DEDICATION**

This book is dedicated to My Legacy
Endia Nicole, Asia Nichele and Osborn IV

YOU ARE THE GIIFTS that I unwrap and return to God daily. Graciously, I was given privileged influence, purposeful right and eternal duty to raise you in His manner. How blessed I am.

As your mom, I remained committed to standing on the front lines - keeping you informed, motivated and safe; all the while modeling the way. As you inhaled, I whispered prayers for your air to be fully purified. As you walked, I asked God to order each of your steps. As you slept, I took note of your dreams and placed them at God's feet for alignment with His will. From this never-ending labor, I have been rewarded *over* and *over* and *over* again.

The journey we have traveled has been long and sometimes a winding, bumpy road. We never gave in to the detours and distractions along the way, but instead kept our compass focused north. Your unwavering trust and unconditional love served as the fuel for my unrelenting engine.

Now learned and equipped, I pray the legacy of greatness you have come to know can be abundantly fulfilled in your lives - and ultimately inspired upon others.

Your first and forever love,
Momzie, Mothership, Mom, respectfully

CONTENTS

FOREWARD	ix
PREFACE	xv

PART ONE | **Our Current Geography**
Chapter 1: The State of our Seed	1
Chapter 2: The Plight of the Farmer	9
Chapter 3: Case Studies	23

PART TWO | **The Blueprints**
Chapter 4: The Legend	33
Chapter 5: The Plan	39
Call to Action	40
The Promise	41
The Consequence	41

PART THREE | **The Field Guide for Parenting**
Chapter 6: Cultivation and Fertilization	47
Chapter 7: Planting	85
Chapter 8: Harvesting	99
Chapter 9: Understanding Seasons	111

PART FOUR | **Advanced Farming**
Chapter 10: Bad Seed	123
Chapter 11: Contemporary Mixed Cropping	125
Chapter 12: The Famine	127

APPENDIX	129

FOREWARD

BY AGE FORTY-SIX, I had been *down the aisle* three times – divorced twice from my children's father and then annulled from a four-year situation (i.e. a 21st century matrimonial mess).

Stay tuned for my future publishing and re-write of this story God transformed from the perfect murder-mystery to another Inspiring and GREAT Moment.

Through all of life's summersaults and roller coaster experiences, my strong relationship with God was never compromised. Having a foundation built on solid principles allowed me to never lose sight of the prize. My prize, was producing *good citizens* and ensuring their success was uninterrupted by the indiscretions of the world around them. With my unseasoned eyes, my immature definition of a good citizen, in time evidenced my understanding of the *call for greatness* in its barest form.

To obtain my prize, I knew that NOTHING - no temptation, addiction, sin, outside influence, lack, personal desire, challenge or disappointment, could be allowed to get in the way. Sacrifice became my middle name and I accepted early that there would likely be few in my corner or on my team along the way. *Nothing* absolutely meant *nothing*.

Then there was life, and as certain as I proclaimed "nothing", EVERYTHING made it's unexpected and restless appearance. I learned quickly that being on-guard did not qualify as being prepared. As a parent, there is no perfect prescription for raising children nor a one-size fits all approach. Fortunately, I discovered a few simple truths that consistently, over time proved to be extremely effective and clearly evidenced. These truths are a combination of biblical teachings, experiences from my own childhood and other basic perennial learnings my elders believed, taught and lived by.

I was married for the first time at age twenty-five; a forward-thinking college graduate with a high aptitude and aspirations to finding stability in a progressive community. I was employed, but had not yet found my career or passion. I didn't have an extreme amount of debt, but I was not actively saving or preparing for a financially secure future. My spouse was of similar status and mindset; six years my senior.

During our 4-year courtship there were many ups and downs, but we pushed them aside and decided to wed despite. We lived away from our home state, so I spent a lot of time long-distance wedding planning and coordinating the events to come. For the most part things were going well, until we discovered a few months prior to the wedding, I was expecting.

I recall visiting my parents and sharing the news. My mom, sitting on my left, was content and relishing slightly in the beauty of the moment. While my dad, sitting to my right, was not the least bit excited or in celebration of the news. My dad was extremely concerned with the image of being pregnant before marriage and us not being in position to take on a new baby so soon after becoming a married couple. Prepared or not, they both understood that there was no other option and grandchild number three was on the way.

Wedding day neared and I traveled to my home state to begin the three-day countdown. My wedding party began to arrive throughout the first day and final to-dos were in motion. The eve of the wedding arrived and after being out all day with my fiancé, I decided to make a call back to my parents to check on things. Little did I know I'd be met with "your mom has been rushed to the emergency room".

My fiancé and I immediately redirected ourselves to the hospital and upon arriving we found out my mother had already been admitted and received a medical diagnosis of AML (acute myeloid leukemia); and a very aggressive form of the disease. Due to the severity of the situation, my mother had already received medical attention and urgently started on chemotherapy treatment.

The day's events cast a dark cloud on all things wedding and the world stopped both its rotation and movement. The last thing on everyone's mind, especially mine, was the wedding event scheduled for the next day. However, my parent's wishes were that the wedding go forth as planned.

What was supposed to be one of my happiest days, turned out to be the saddest; a day frozen in time. My plan was for my mother to be with me as I stepped into my wedding gown. My plan was for my mom to be escorted down the aisle to her reserved seat on the front pew. My plan was for her to be equally as beautiful and gleaming in the many photos from my wedding day. It became apparent, that God had a completely different plan.

I can recall physically standing at the altar, but mentally being at the hospital. I remember being completely dazed at the reception and greeting guests with a weak, half-hearted smile. All the while, I was daydreaming about leaving the reception to be with my mom across the bridge in her hospital room. After the last item on the program ended, the entire wedding party and my immediate family loaded up the limousines and transitioned the gathering to my mother's bedside. When we arrived, my mom was resting, but immediately became elated by our presence. To make the moment more special, my uncle brought along his video camera so that my mom could view the ceremony recording and feel like she was a part of the big day.

Six months after the wedding, I gave birth to a baby girl. She was by far the apple, peach and plum of my mother's eye. At the time, my mother was in remission and having her first granddaughter gave her new life. She played in my daughter's soft, curly hair and pampered her as if she were her very own. There were several moments I believe my mom forgot that I gave birth to her.

Sadly, eleven months after my daughter's birth, my mother's battle with leukemia and her life ended. Her death left an enormous void in our entire family and forever changed the construct of how we related to each other. Her missed smile alone exposed darkened spaces we didn't quite know how to respond to. She was the glue and we were all forced to figure out how to keep things together without her guidance or input.

Life continued and six months after my mom's passing, I birthed daughter number two. In the latter months of my mother's life, we'd made plans for her to be present and enjoy both granddaughters, but unfortunately our plan was not fulfilled. In the in-between moments when my daughters were born, in addition to losing my mom, my husband and I separated and initiated the formal divorce process. This period of my life became known as 3D – death, delivery and divorce. Fortunately, over time, a different combination of D's got me thru – discernment, deliverance and dominion. I learned that the former D's were offered to me by the world, but God gifted me with the latter.

God never professed that life on earth would be trouble-free. He did however, promise to always be present and be our burden bearer. Through all the painful moments of my life and interruptions to the blissful dreams of grandeur, what remained consistent and untampered was my personal conviction and commitment to my children – providing them stability, giving them an abundance of love, and fully sacrificing my wants for their needs.

Divorce and death brought temporary dark clouds, but eventually the sun arose. The desolate moments came and they went. They struck a blow and left behind dual memories of both sadness and victory. Most notable is that no separation ever came to my daughters and me. Wherever I was, so were they. The sacrifice I made to be fully engaged and completely responsive to my girls, despite what life brought to our door, came with no regrets.

This time taught me forgiveness, love, joy, peace, patience, generosity, modesty, faithfulness, and self-control. What others may have perceived as my season of loneliness and despair, turned out to be a period of exponential growth and wisdom development. Not at first appreciating, I came to recognize that I had been chosen to participate in a higher learning course focused on the fruits of the Holy Spirit[1]. Thus, what was plotted for evil against me, God turned into good[2].

Years passed, and my ex-husband and I reacquainted, remarried and eventually gave birth to a son. Several *everything's* again surfaced during the course of our new relationship, including challenges with my

---

[1] The Holy Bible, Galatians 5:22-23

[2] The Holy Bible, Genesis 5:20

health, but each experience propelled me to a higher place on my journey. In the oddest of ways, my life depicted the evolution of a seed being planted, cultivated and maturing to full ripeness over time; then used to bring sustenance to others – over and over again.

My ripeness occurred after several hot, cold and transitioning seasons – all with challenges, but never impeding the ability to prosper and grow. Occasionally, I found myself amidst *weeds and disease carrying and destructive predators*, but fortunately by God's grace and the support of several field soldiers, I remained protected and flourished. From my personal experiences, I lived out the specific lessons and principles by which to raise my own children.

The parallel symmetry between the psychology of parenting and the fundamentals of farming were quite remarkable. The interchangeable connotation of terms like seed, sow, reap, harvest evidenced there was intentional purpose embedded in the science of farming. I began to seek God for clarity, and became a student of scripture and agricultural concepts.

Now those understandings are presented in this book as a roadmap for inspiring generational greatness. I believe strongly that by tapping into the concepts of farming, we can better grasp the key behaviors and steps for preparing, planting, and nourishing our children to greatness.

This book is intended to provide a thorough description of each farming principle, offering biblical reference and sharing practical interpretation and real-life expression for direct application. It is the goal of this book to provide instruction, intervention and support for all families – in hopes of cultivating a generation of greatness, one seed at a time.

PREFACE

Current state analysis is not just an effective business process. Even in the realm of parenting, the strategic plan to understand the truth as it is, and not as it is assumed, is also a pivotal step in planning toward desired results. Considering the many dimensions of a child and the world around them, there is much to review and analyze. Every decision we make as a parent has a life-long consequence. Thus, to ensure we have an effective path-forward we must become extremely disciplined in the art of *evaluating where we are* and *responding accordingly* – and doing so with a sense of urgency.

The leading contributor to most parents not performing this step is not because they don't care, it's the inability to envision and stay focused on the desired results. Some of the questions parents have been unable to answer include – What purpose was my child birthed for and how will my child contribute to the world? How do I want my child to relate to others? What areas of my child's life need to be different from mine? What measures do I need to take to ensure my child is flourishing and their environment is conducive to such? Though most parents don't fully answer these questions, their intent is not minimized. The timing and state of things strongly suggests however, we need to move from *intent* to **action**.

In the chapters ahead, we will explore the present outlook of our children and the challenges facing parents today. Before we can begin discussing solutions, we must have a clear perspective of our current reality. In our day-to-day lives when we experience (or even hear about) negative or painful situations caused by our children, we don't often pause to understand the drivers for the behavior or contributors to the poor decision making. Due to this lack of inquiry, we are actually doing more to further the bad behavior than influencing or inspiring change.

Silence and inaction in these situations is a sign of indifference.

Admitting that we don't have a clear sense of what is, also expresses the sentiment that we don't understand what or how large the gap between *what is* and *what should be* really is. With this being said, we can't officially proclaim how little or much remediation is needed to win our children back and get them on a path to greatness. This degree of uncertainty is unhealthy, and must be responded to with haste.

As you read, you are encouraged to journal or take notes of any revelation you have. It will be very interesting to see how many of your thoughts are validated along the way. More importantly, you will be surprised at how a simple shift in perspective opens the door to action and allows for a greater impact in the lives of our children and the generations to come.

PART ONE
Our Current Geography

CHAPTER 1
THE STATE OF OUR SEED

It comes as no surprise the epidemic facing our children and future generations. What we see, hear and personally face are enough to conclude that our seed (ie. children) are an irreversible fail. More concerningly, some have already accepted this as the ultimate reality and thus have ceased trying to understand the problem or influence change.

The state of our seed could also be defined by the extreme statistics on juvenile crime or sharing events from the many disheartening news headlines across the country. However, there is not much to be accomplished by increasing our competency on these unpleasant data outcomes. To have true realization of the predicament facing our children, we will have to invoke an intense level of hindsight, reflection and awareness; which is the objective of this book's opening chapters.

Traveling to this deep, inward, often unvisited place will challenge you to proceed in reading with an *as-long-as-it-takes pause then proceed*, instead of a *hurried, page turn and read* approach. The value of this writing comes when we allow for purposeful meditation and divine instruction to saturate our mental being.

Starting this intense journey begins with validating some of our thoughts against reality. Ask yourself, "what are the top 3 juvenile crimes, offenses or violations?". Feel free to record your responses in the space provided.

1.

2.

3.

Once you have the crimes, offenses or violations in mind or listed above, select one of them and then think about, or scribe below a response to each question,

A1. What decision-making steps or preparatory questions *likely* took place before the juvenile offender committed the crime, offense or violation?

B1. How much consideration did the juvenile offender *likely* give to the consequences of their decision?

Next, consider the following questions assuming a 'best self' perspective for the same crime, offense or violation you selected above.

A2. What decision-making steps and/or preparatory questions *should have* taken place before the juvenile offender commits the crime, offense or violation?

B2. How much consideration *should* the juvenile offender have given to the consequences of their decision?

For a complete list of the top 25 Crimes, Offense, and Violations see the Appendix.

Now completing the questions from both a 'what was likely' and 'what should be' state of mind, take some time to analyze and acknowledge the differences between the two. A sample response and gap analysis is shown.

Questions A1/A2: Decision Making Steps		
A1. Likely	A2. Should Be	Gap Analysis
Will I get what I want right now and not have to spend any money?	Is stealing the right thing to do? Will I be better off because I have stolen this object? Who could I be hurting if I steal this object? How can I obtain this object the right way and how long would it take? What will happen if I get caught? How could getting caught hurt me (and those who love me) now and in the future?	Juvenile Offender appears to only focus on potential positive outcomes and how it will benefit them. There is no concern for others or realization that their decision could impact them as well, short term and long term. They don't appear to consider the true value of what they could obtain versus what they could lose.

Questions B1/B2: Consideration of Consequences		
B1. Likely	B2. Should Be	Gap Analysis
Minimal; don't think I'll get caught.	A great deal; consequences matter and can impact today and the future – not to mention cause issues and grief for others	Juvenile Offender is focused only on the reward and either does not realize or care about the likely loss, problems or discord their decision would cause.

Based on the brief exercise above, an argument could be made that the dilemma facing the juvenile offender is a derivative of lacking empathy and/or lacking a sense of reality. While both may be true, the root of the dilemma goes much further than the absence of basic emotion or facts. Additionally, even in the example above where no demographics are offered, there is no apparent variation in the behavior and decisions made based on the personal profile of the juvenile offender. It is this truth that introduces us to the initial study on the condition of our seed.

Children come in all colors, shapes and sizes, from many different cultures, neighborhoods and ethnicities, but their actions are more justified based on less divisive characteristics. The age of a child, coupled with the influences of their background, is more the driver of how they think and respond. More plainly, the predicament facing and behaviors exhibited by preschoolers will be quite different than those of pre-teen age children. Which then contradicts societal beliefs that children of a single race, ethnicity or community are carbon copies of each other. With this, we will explore the state of our seed categorically by age and circumstance.

Understanding the Ages

<u>0 - 5 years</u>

Children in this age group are extremely impressionable and are more like a sponge than a brush. The behaviors observed will in most cases be a mimicking of what they have seen, with little rationale or meaning behind it. Decisions, like the learned behaviors, are also not founded on much reasoning, if any at all. At this age, consequences are not necessarily understood, though the foundation of what they are should definitely be in motion. This is the age that will less likely be an offender, but beginning signs may be present in areas that have absorbed some negative impact or influence.

6 - 10 years

In this age range, children have typically developed a sense of self, have formed a personality and a fact-less basis for the way they think. How they behave at this age is both learned and observed from those around them. The sphere of influence is greater at this age because there is more exposure to television, electronic media, other school age children – all added with the fact that they may be spending more time alone. Unless taught in the younger years, the idea of consequences may be farthest from their accepted reality. Children at this age begin to have an increased desire for "what they want" and thus begin to more consistently test the waters.

The pushing limits schema is well thought out. The 6-10 year old sensors activate on demand to determine the best path to *get what they want, gauge how far they can go without getting caught* and *knowing what manipulations work in keeping them out of trouble*. Considering the junior nature of their behavior in their parent's eye, the bad choices they make are often ignored or explained away. Often parents will describe this as "cute" or say, "they are just children". With this, children in this age range become programmed for bad decision making and advanced, bad behavior.

11 - 15 years (or older)

Though barely teen-agers, children at this age who have matured thru undisciplined moments where correction was warranted and necessary, are prime candidates for juvenile crime. The behaviors that have now become progressive did not just show up. By the time a child reaches this age, they have built their own database of tested behaviors, trends, practices and thoughts that all contribute to who they have now become.

The most surprising change at this age however, is that the poor choices and bad behavior, which in most cases surfaced long ago, are met with legal and/or escalated response. To the child's surprise, they become confused, more frustrated and often enraged, because the intervention is happening in a manner that is inconsistent with what they experienced in the past. This is a risky age to *begin* parenting, as the work to teach proper mental agility, clear thinking and appropriate reply and reaction is an upward and arduous climb.

The above characterization paints a scantly, yet finished painting of our children positioned for failure. Though not hopeless, they are certainly less promising of greatness without immediate intervention. Our children, even thru their most despicable, unthinkable and tragic moments, are screaming for help and attention. This cry unfortunately, is often confronted by an instinctive silence, blame shifting or unclaimed responsibility.

Mom, Dad, Family, Teacher, Neighbor and Friend- we must acknowledge the truth and face the light. Despite what archaeologists say, our seed – today's and tomorrow's – are the world's most endangered species. Unless we change our action and response, complete moral decline and extinction become the unplanned plan.

In comparison

Worth acknowledging, there are many children that naturally thrive and represent GREATNESS with little effort. Children of this likeness have a strong ability to make good decisions and lead a positive, fruitful life. In these cases, upon traceback and analysis of their life's events and circumstances, the degree of greatness in their lineage or immediate surroundings could be validated and argued to be the source of reason. These children too, are also a variation of seed that have been dually sown with fervent prayer and divine covering.

CONSIDER

A single day's news broadcast with no crime or mischief to report.

- What feelings are you experiencing?
- What thoughts are coming to mind as you replay this in your mind?
- What do you suppose our youth are doing in lieu of committing a crime or offense?
- What do you think is on the mind of a child that is now taking part in the new, positive activity?
- What do you suspect could have contributed to the change in activity – from the child's perspective? Yours and the community?
- How has the world around you changed and what do you think is the news story of the day?

Because a crime-free day is so far from reality, our minds may have difficulty sketching such an imagined phenomenon. Due to this, we must go deeper than a review of the external and place emphasis on the internal emotions and triggers, feelings and motivations – for both our seed and ourselves.

No decision or action occurs without influence from our conscious and unconscious state of mind. How we feel and perceive, directly impact everything we think and do. Therefore, to understand the state of our seed, is to understand how they feel and see.

Some would say we have reached a place of no return and having hope is a lost cause. Interestingly, this outlook is correct if immediate, drastic – yet sincere – intervention does not take place. If we improve upon our understandings and personal accountabilities, and then reconnect and pursue an honest, stern and consistent relationship with our children, we are more than capable of inspiring them to greatness.

> *Your awe-inspiring deeds will be on every tongue;*
> *I will proclaim your greatness.*
> Psalms 145:6

What is Greatness?
What does being great look like? Is great the same as perfect?

The nature and definition of greatness is broad in nature, but can be surmised to emphasize the energy, time, attitude, and consistency put into making good decisions and pushing past perceived circumstances. This manner of being is quite remarkable. By exhibiting this power, one would not be labeled as perfect, but the thoughtful manner in which they live develops them into a contagious, creative and inspiring being, otherwise known as *great*. This being is the seed that would exist, flourish and then reproduce generations of greatness, one planted seed at a time.

Greatness is not defined by how fewer times one does wrong, but how infrequently one does the same thing wrong. Greatness is having power over oneself; learning from a mistake and having self-control to not repeat it. Greatness is considerate of others and thoughtfully experiencing life wearing another's shoes. Greatness is seeing thru the lens of others, but never having a blind eye to what's right. Greatness is expecting the best, but being understanding, tolerant and appropriately responsive when met with the worst. Greatness is inside beauty that lives out loud. Greatness is the lightest of light that penetrates thru the darkest of dark.

This greatness, despite what it appears to be and speaking in the affirmative**, *is the state of our seed.***

CHAPTER 2
THE PLIGHT OF THE FARMER

The farmer plants seed by taking God's word to others.
Mark 4:14

Just like a farmer, a parent is the individual responsible for nurturing and raising a seed to harvest. In both roles, there is a considerable charge and accountability to plant, birth and mature. As so, the terms and naming will be used interchangeably throughout this book and is the thematic basis and essence of **Inspired|Legacy**.

The perspective of this book also extends the term parent to include the variety of individuals that have an intimate level of relations with your child and have influence, personal responsibility and impact on them. It is common for people in this sphere to have vested interest in your child's future and provide nurturing and correction. Thus, accepting the viewpoint that "it takes a village to raise a child" helps emphasize the critical need to monitor and be very selective about who is around and in your child's life.

The parenting village can often include both biological parents, and at times only one or neither, in cases of adoption or foster parenting. This structuring however, despite what the world would lead us to believe, does not have any merit on the outcome and level of greatness a child can grow to become. For years, statistics have portrayed children of divorce as hopeless and helpless; and that falsehood offers great ammunition to be proven otherwise. It's not the who, it's the what and how. This book is filled with the needed information and techniques to support all parents and parenting structures in the quest to inspire their seed to greatness - and continue for generations to come.

The simplest requirements to cultivating greatness in your child are first having a full understanding of what it means to be great, pursuing it in your own life and then inspiring your child to model the same. Notably within these requirements, there is no condition statement that concludes being a married couple guarantees achievement of greatness. Stating this, however, is not intended to contradict the sanctity of marriage and God's plan in directing a couple to be fruitful, and multiply[3]. God certainly instructs the best-case scenario and He would want a child to be brought into the world and raised by a loving, righteous set of parents.

Alternatively, God's overwhelming message of love overshadows the parent relationship status and clearly demonstrates deference to the relations from individual to individual. Thus, a child being nurtured to greatness – even if it is by way of one, strong, God-fearing, God-loving parent would prove to be more effective and welcomed.

Regardless of how many parents, we will approach parenting from an individual context, as each parent has their own role, impact and responsibility. While one parent may be doing all the right things, their efforts could be thwarted by the counterproductive efforts of the other. As parents, we don't set out to fail our children, and in most cases, we don't recognize that we are. For this reason, to have a complete measurement of reality, assessing the state of our children will require a complete study of our own implied and expressed behaviors.

More than DNA is passed on to our children. Everything we think, do, feel and experience has the potential to show up in our child's life. We often think that our children aren't paying attention or are miraculously shielded from our personal experiences. Not true. The negative and most minimal of events, the most buried emotions and secrets of our past take residence on the spiritual train and arrive at unexpected stops along our child's journey. Hence, understanding the state of the farmer, requires a

---

[3] The Holy Bible, Genesis 1:28

fully transparent and introspective examination of *all things* YOU.

This self-evaluation is dual focused and begins with an understanding of unresolved issues, buried emotions or fears that unknowingly serve as trigger points for negative interactions with your child. These unintentional behaviors occur as a derivative of past experiences that are obscure, hidden or completely subconscious; which until realized can be very harmful to a child's development. These behaviors will be termed Indirect Affects (IA).

Indirect Affects (IA)

Parents, and all persons for that matter, experience difficult and troubling situations. These moments can lead to harbored feelings and emotions, sometimes for a short duration or even a lifetime. In addition, we all face circumstances that stem from our own wretchedness and poor decision making. Whether it is family conflict, relationship drama, drug or alcohol addiction, sexual sin, having a deceitful tongue or exhibiting any lack of self-control - we all have some form of a blemish – some visible to the world, some not. Some have struggled with the same issue for many years, while others have been delivered from one and now face the challenge of another. The struggle to be righteous in our ways is *real*.

This struggle, as real as it is, inhibits our growth, success and greatness. More so, the impact to our children is even more abundant. The danger in not overcoming our issues and setbacks, prior to entering the land of parenting, introduces the likelihood of either setting a bad example for our children, representing true hypocrisy in saying one thing and doing another, or completely slacking in our responsibility because the sin, unfortunate moment or negative behavior overwhelms us. These behaviors, individually and in total, are very common and damaging realities.

Thus, the best recourse in minimizing the impact to your child is to seek immediate support and complete healing. Along with issue management, especially if you are already a parent, using the *struggle* as the basis for "truth parenting" with your child can prove extremely effective. Truth parenting is a concept defined by open, honest, and genuine communication between parents and children, substituting weakness and pretense with strength and character. Unbeknownst to many, children crave parental guidance – and this is made easier when they are privy to your imperfections and journey to greatness. This concept will be discussed further in *Chapter 6 – Cultivation and Fertilization*.

Recognizing that you may have some difficulty identifying your Indirect Affects, it is recommended that you take a quiet and extended pause to review the following questions. Your approach in answering the questions should be uninhibited, free of judgement or condemnation and forgiving of yourself and others. Your focus should be on the mountain of blessings you gain by climbing the foothills of your past. At this stage, all the *everything's* of yesterday need to become the *nothing's* of your tomorrow.

Indirect Affects (IA) Self-Assessment Questions

- Do you have any secrets that if known by your child, parents or closest friends, would completely change their image of who you are or introduce a completely contrasting persona of you?

- Is there any situation that initiates a negative response or energy when mentioned, remembered or unintentionally repeated?

- Is there any individual that you would consider an enemy?

- Is there anyone you have not forgiven or have unresolved issues with?

- Is there anyone that you have not appropriately emotionally detached from that is no longer in your life?

- Is there any habit, behavior or activity that you do that you would not want your child to repeat?

- Is there any habit, behavior or activity that you feel a sense of guilt before, during or after it's done?

- Are there any past decisions made that changed the course of your life for the 'worse' that you have not recovered from?

- Do you have any regrets that may be negatively influencing your decisions today?

If you answered Yes to any of the above questions, it is highly probable that you are *infected* and *contagious*, and likely to be displacing an Indirect Affect upon your child. If the IA can be easily identified, you are well on your way to changing the behavior because understanding differently allows for you to behave differently. In these recognizable areas seeking help to gain better clarity would be a great benefit to you and your child.

Alternatively, if you answered Yes to any of the questions above but cannot identify the issue or understand the actual Indirect Affect, the next best step is to immediately engage in counseling or find a reliable, proven resource to talk to and develop a healing plan. Assuming you were completely open and provided the most truthful responses, it is probable that there are deeper-rooted feelings and emotions that will require additional exploration. In light of this, the remaining concepts of this book will not prove effective or be long-lasting until awareness is obtained and healing begins. Any positive strides to be made with your child must originate from *your state of great*.

If a more prolonged pause is necessary - take it. Bettering yourself is the greatest gift you could give to yourself and your child. In the interim, enlisting the help of others to assist in creating a positive environment for your child is a compromising way to initiate the *great* movement.

Surround yourself and your child with greatness and allow it to manifest in and around you both. Allow what's in your midst to inspire you toward ultimate healing and deliverance.

> *As iron sharpens iron, so one person sharpens another.*
> Proverbs 27:17

Direct Effects (DE)

The second phase of your self-evaluation is to formally identify with the manifestations of the Indirect Affects. Understanding how open wombs of your past, show up and impact your child and the parent-child relationship are key. These behaviors can be physical and/or verbal in nature, but most distinguishable by the immediate impact to and response from your child. Hence, these behaviors are termed Direct Effects (DE). The damage from Direct Effects can be instantaneous or slow-building. In either case, having full awareness and then correcting the Indirect Affects remains the critical breakthrough needed to ignite greatness in yourself and your child.

To grasp the correlation between Indirect Affects (IA) and Direct Effects (DE), a few *unfortunately* common parent-to-child relationship illustrations are provided. Each illustration provides insight into the behavioral cause and effect, and a view of the behaviors essential to and exhibited in the *great* state.

Illustration 1: Having little to no interest or engagement

Distracted by the many adversities life brings, parents can often become self-absorbed or simply overcome with worry, doubt or fear of the future. Due to this positioning, there is little room for an actual relationship between the parent and child, let alone a positive one. Hence, the parent must quickly resolve the barriers that are impeding a focused, attentive and loving environment for the child to be raised in.

Children look to their parents for many things – approval, guidance, security, support; just to name a few. When a child is not receiving these things, they will eventually lose drive, purpose and interest. This then opens the door for them to become removed and susceptible to influences not in their best interest; which ultimately interrupts and redirects their intended path.

The alternative and recommendation is that we be ever-present, ever-concerned, ever-interested, ever-encouraging and ever-understanding. As parents, we should never stop or be remiss in teaching, offering of wisdom and insisting on togetherness with our child. A child should always feel that they are important and a priority. This feeling creates a deep affection and compassion for others that has long-term reward, as your child repeats this behavior with their own children.

> *Real Life Expression*
>
> Being a single parent, I cannot recall very many events or important moments in my child's life I wasn't fully present. Fully present goes beyond just sitting in the same room. It's being informed and aware of the before, the during and the after. At a very young age, I instilled a business-like concept with my children called 'debriefing'. Debriefing was the time between my child arriving home from school and dinner. Unless it was absolutely unavoidable, I stopped everything (even rescheduled meetings) to check in with each child. Our check-in time would include anything from what they ate at lunch to what didn't go right during the day and how could it have been better.
>
> Due to this debriefing, I became fortunate to learn a lot about my children. At any moment, I could name their friends (and foes), clearly articulate what their triggers were - positive and negative - and identify the reasons behind their varying moods.
>
> Though this debriefing time benefited me, an equal benefit was for my child. First it evidenced how important they were to me and how their needs superseded anything the world needed from me. Secondly, my

> children had a level of comfort with me that I wasn't going to judge a situation, yet instead seek to first understand and then reach a fair assessment and solution together. Thirdly, though not in final, my children sought and trusted what I had to say.
>
> As years passed, my children grew to expect this time, and on occasion impatiently waited for them to commence. I knew that my children were inspired by my wisdom. They appreciated my logical method of approaching situations, and doing so in a positive, realistic manner. As much as they kept me informed, the exercise also served as a valuable learning experience to benefit them current day and in the future.

Illustration 2: Abusive

Hurt people, hurt people – simply put. The entire premise of a Direct Effect is that some past hurt, emotion or fear is triggered and deferred. Relative to abusive situations, due to the possible extremity and alarming affects, escalated attention should be given to any Indirect Affect having any form of abusive activity. It is dangerous and irresponsible to not attend to and find solace from these feelings in haste. If not, ownership of a child's failures and sinister acts reside in the space of your *aged un-resolve.*

Abuse can come in the form of verbal attacks, like extreme shouting, comparing, shaming, labeling, or physical harm – which can include sexual and non-sexual. In all, abuse is any violent or cruel treatment towards another; especially when done repeatedly or regularly. Though no form of poor treatment is acceptable, being abusive is the most detestable because in every abusive moment, the lasting effects are multiplied and often irreversible.

There is not much that has to be said about physical harm, due to the obvious injury and nature of the act. So, for the sake of bringing light to the other forms of abusive offense to a child, we will explore them a bit further.

Extreme shouting/Yelling

A name shout or stern command to get your child's attention may be warranted occasionally, but should never be the norm. Constant communication in this manner makes a child fearful and grow numb to instruction. This communication style ignites rebellion, anxiety, low self-esteem and an unwillingness to cooperate or succumb to authority.

Though yelling may appear to just be an audible disturbance, it actually produces psychological and medical damage. For years, studies have been done on the effects of yelling at children and the results have resoundingly shown that harsh verbal discipline increased depression and other poor behaviors[4]. For many of us, we grew up in households where yelling was common practice and thus we assumed the same communication style with our own children. Though not typically recognized as problematic, the penetrating and long-lasting effects of receiving this treatment is likely suppressed and mislabeled something else.

It is more difficult to diagnose verbal abuse than other forms of mistreatment. However, if we did an honest assessment, we may be able to replay the explosive moments of the past, connect with how we felt – and ultimately acknowledge that our current thoughts, beliefs and emotions were somehow shaped around those experiences.

Considering all of this, there is nothing positive that can come from communicating in this manner. Thus, as discussed with Indirect Affects, it is important to unearth the situations in your life that are contributing

---

[4] "Harsh Verbal Discipline Just As Bad As Physical Punishment", accessed February 11, 2018. ttps://www.redorbit.com/news/health/1112939307/harsh-verbal-discipline-as-bad-as-physical-punishment-090413/

to this Direct Effect and resolve them with a sense of urgency.

Comparing/Shaming/Labeling

This Direct Effect often goes unnoticed and sometimes requires someone external to the situation to call attention to it. This communicative style is typically engrained and not easily identifiable in day-to-day conversation. It is somewhat second nature and habitual. Constantly making references to another sibling or individual in a manner that identifies lack in your child, telling your child what they are not or specifically calling them a derogatory name are all extremely destructive behaviors. These actions collectively can also be characterized as verbal abuse.

For example, a parent may call their child selfish or lazy on a daily basis and never realize they are officially labeling their child. This labeling tells your child that they are less than and offers the child no path to getting better. In turn, the child begins to see themselves as only the lacking behavior and ultimately proves the labeling to be true. Additional impacts, like low self-esteem, poor social skills, lack of drive, poor decision making, and even depression present themselves.

Calling attention to your child being lazy or unproductive is one thing, affirming who they are based on the behavior is another. Effective parenting is a balance between loving, teaching and disciplining – and when this is executed properly, the negative impacts to our children is minimized and we author in the cultivation of greatness we were charged to do.

As with the previous sections, understanding what triggers this behavior is imperative to your ability to be a nurturing parent. You may have been able to trace this back to labels you had or disproportionate comparisons made between you and some other person that impacted your psyche and how you feel about yourself. Like yelling, behaviors we endured often become the behaviors we repeatedly express. Recognizing where the counterproductive behavior lives in our being and ridding it is critically important. If necessary, getting help for yourself is the critical next best step.

Illustration 3: No discipline/consequence or consistent discipline executed when warranted

The associated Indirect Affect could be one of two extremes – being over-disciplined or being un-disciplined. Depending on the household you experienced, you developed your style and preferred manner of discipline from your feelings and response to the punishing methods executed by your parent(s). Considering you chose to not discipline or teach your children the importance of consequences, it is safe to assume that you did not at minimum find value in the same.

Speaking from experience, it can be tough to issue or maintain a punishment on your child. Because you share such a bond with them, you often feel like you are punishing yourself when you punish your child. Unpleasant as it may be, we must separate the roles and as the parent, teach our children discipline and that every action has a consequence. There aren't many things in this world that don't have rules or guidelines attached. From board games to busy highways and roads, boundaries are established to prevent chaos, confusion and harm; while creating order, structure and safety.

When we choose to allow our children to live a limitless, unruly life the results can be catastrophic. Coming to their defense in warranted situations is one thing, but to constantly intervene in situations where your child was wrong and violated a rule, does them more harm than good. Also, not being firm in instances when a punishment is rendered, has a back-firing potential as well. When children aren't taught the value of rules and are allowed to disregard them or be held fully accountable for their actions, you are leaving a great deal of room for unpredictable, disaster.

> *"He who spares the rod hates his son, but he who loves him is careful to discipline him."*
> Proverbs 13:24

Discipline and instruction are essential to effective parenting. Children who grow up in undisciplined households feel as though they are not valued or cared for. These children lack self-control and direction, thus create their own path, rules and limitations. As these children age, they often rebel and have little or no respect for any kind of authority, including God's.

Thus, parenting without discipline and consequences is a recipe for disaster. Understandably, no parent wants to see their child experience pain, but in situations where the consequence brings forth significant growth and long-lasting wisdom – the value far exceeds the cost.

Illustration 4: Lying for/on behalf of the child; and the child is aware

Taboo to some, but the act and use of the word "lie" should be an accepted norm. If something said is untrue, it is a lie. A growingly common Direct Effect is demonstrating blatant deceit by lying for or on behalf of our child, and doing so in the presence of the child. From personally observing this, it is obvious that the lying parent thinks they are protecting their child or doing them a favor to misrepresent the truth in the eyes of someone else. This fallacy could not be the furthest from the truth.

This behavior, in its most fundamental state shows your child that you don't value the truth. It tells your child that being honest is not a necessary or worthy trait to have and again that suffering consequences is not a worthwhile fate. Unlike the biblical principle that 'the truth will set you free'[5], we are teaching our children thru this behavior that the bondage of a lie is safer.

It's frightening and frankly, very disheartening to believe that there are parents that lie for or on behalf of their children, but it is even more terrifying when they do it in front of their children. This is abuse in and of itself. What gain is there to befriend our child and build this strong, united and supportive bond all based on a foolishly weak and fragile, foundation? This is without question a self-destructing matter and the starter to an inextinguishable fire.

The expressions of love toward our child go a very long way. This love builds a foundation that can withstand the most unrestrained situations and a wall to lean on if and when the weight becomes too heavy to bear. Thus, in parenting situations where we must introduce discipline the child should be made to understand that the punishment is *coupled with love*. Parents should always side on the side of honesty and correctness; even when the consequences carry a heavy toll. These moments serve as very important teaching moments and instill character and strength - which both lead to a path of greatness.

---

[5] The Holy Bible, John 8:32

CHAPTER 3
CASE STUDIES

To further demonstrate the commingled relationship between the seed and the farmer, and obtain a better perspective of the importance in addressing the Indirect Affects and Direct Effects, several Case Studies will be reviewed below. Each Case Study will (1) describe the Plight of the Farmer, (2) identify potential Indirect Affects, (3) identify potential Direct Effects, and (4) discuss the State of the Seed – (a) how they are impacted by the IA/DE and (b) their actual state of being.

Scenarios with extreme issues like abuse, alcohol/drug addiction, and sexual assault are not included, as the impact and path towards a healthy relationship and parenting structure are greater and potentially severe. These situations should immediately be directed to a professional and/or spiritual counselor.

**Due to the unique nature of family relationships formed by way of adoption, discussion on this topic will be limited, although it is likely techniques discussed in this book may be relatable and useful*

Case Study 1:

The Farmer's Plight:

Long-time dating couple, often breaking up over issues that make it hard to trust each other. No evidence of infidelity, but suspected by one mate. The couple has a 3-year-old child.

Potential Indirect Affects:

- Couple has lack of trust and respect for each other
- Couple not loving each other fully
- Couple is unforgiving of each other's past mistakes

Potential Direct Effects
- Child intermittently ignored or not given proper attention

The State of the Seed:

This situation is very common and could vary over what the unresolved issues are between the couple, however the impact to the child will mostly be the same. In an environment where a couple is struggling with trust, respect, and unforgiveness, a child will experience intermittent periods of loneliness and confusion, receive inconsistent messages from each parent and not feel as connected as they should to either parent or the family unit.

It is not purposeful, but in this particular case, the parents are likely consumed by the back and forth and incomplete nature of their relationship. They have their own periods of feeling alone, confused, and disconnected. Human behavior is rather predictable, especially when one has not mastered the art of managing emotions or battling the mind – which is best expressed as *where the mind goes, so does the energy*.

Though this couple may care for each other very deeply, love each other the best 'how they love' each other kind of way and have great intention to be a family for life, if the elements causing the Indirect Affects are not dealt with, the probability for relationship and parenting failure are high.

Because the child is 3 years of age does not lessen the impact of the Direct Effects. At this stage, it is very important to resolve the issues before the child gets older, has greater and different needs and requires additional attention. In the long run, it is very likely that the child grows to be either distant, emits mixed messages, never commits or understands how to find, give or receive love. Neither of which is the gift we want to give to our child.

Case Study 2:

The Farmer's Plight:

Divorced couple with unfinished issues or open wombs from the past. One/Both parents already dating someone else and the new mate is not fond of the ex-spouse. The children reside with the biological mother. The divorced couple has 4 children, ages 19, 16, 11 and 5.

Potential Indirect Affects

- Couple resents each other
- Couple has lack of respect for each other
- Couple is unforgiving of each other
- Couple unable to communicate with each other and maintain composure

Potential Direct Effects
- Child intermittently ignored or not given proper attention
- Children are resentful towards their parents' new mate
- Children are disconnected from parents and withhold communications

The State of the Seed:

This situation is also very common and could again vary in the specifics around the grievances facing this couple. Regardless of the actual issues, the impact to the child will bear extreme likeness. In an atmosphere where there is deep-rooted resentment and constant disagreement between the parents, a child cannot flourish. Instead the child will always be seeking a single platform to develop from, a secure place to fit in, and ultimately a stable love story to rest on.

The intent of this couple is not to ignore the needs of their children or give them less than the best parenting. It is unfortunately an element of human nature however, to fight for ourselves first. Thus, when in odds with someone – even if it is a co-parent – most will selfishly choose to pursue their own stance with the co-parent over arriving at a peaceful compromise for the sake of the children.

With the varying ages of the children, there are many things of consideration. Children under age 6 are extremely impressionable and have a keen sense of observation. They are always tuned into what's happening around them. They mimic what they see and will have amazing recall as they get older. It is very important to protect this younger age group as they will - sometimes silently - mature to a very undesirable state and remain under the radar.

From the perspective of the pre-teen and teen, depending on how much they have witnessed, they are extremely confused and likely to have immediate resentments that show up in school and home. This is the danger zone you want to avoid because they are no longer children that you can sway with a sweet treat or in-between-things hug. The energy and time needed to evaluate, understand and restore a child in this age group could be years long.

The other alarming fact of note is that pre-teens and teens are already making plans and calculating their life-after they are no longer in your home. It is extremely likely that they have infused the Indirect Affects into what they think is appropriate and works. They aren't old enough to recognize how far off base their thinking is so the 'great' generation you hoped for is again an improbable reality.

The 19-year-old, alternatively, is in a hit or miss state; especially dependent on how many of their formative years were impacted. The 19-year-old has had time or is at a time of great exposure to many people and ideals from outside your home as well. If these influences are greater and less positive than what was displayed in the home, the journey to recovery is more difficult. However, with the same impact, a child that has self-developed an internal "great" meter can potentially rebound. Unfortunately, even this can be situational and not consistent, because the child was not afforded the opportunity to witness or live this out for themselves. Thus, their staying power and long suffering will have a short stay.

Over time, if resolution nor an agree-to-disagree arrangement is reached between the divorced parents, all four children will adopt the same unagreeable and uncompromising behaviors demonstrated by their parents. As previously discussed, depending on the age of the child, the level of impact can be greater when the Indirect Affects are factored in. In all, everyone suffers and ends up less "great" than they were destined to be when they are under the influence of counterproductive thoughts and behaviors.

Reflection and Reminder

Assessing where we are as parents is a critical component to planning out any next steps with improving life for our children. We cannot make life better for our children until we improve the condition of our own. This book does not profess to provide steps to becoming a perfect parent, but instead serve as a mind-altering catalyst for reshaping our parental perspectives and behaviors.

Worth reminding, our calling as parents is not as onerous and complicated as some may think. Our responsibility is technically limited to – (1) teaching and governing our children in kindness, (2) disciplining our children, (3) providing for our children and (4) setting an example for our children. These responsibilities are explained best and confirmed within several verses of scriptural text. Experience has proven that if these 4 responsibilities are strongly adhered to, the probability of a positive outcome is greatly increased.

Contrary to popular belief, the many extras parents add into the equation or offer in lieu of the prescribed duties – like buying expensive clothes or giving in to every whim of their child – does not fit into the model God set forth, nor add anything to the value of the seed. Consider what happens to a seed plant that is over-watered?

Below are a few scripture references that can serve as instruction, motivation and confirmation.

Teach them toward righteousness and govern them in kindness

Fathers, do not provoke your children to anger, but bring them up in the discipline and instruction of the Lord.
Ephesians 6:4

And these words that I command you today shall be on your heart. You shall teach them diligently to your children, and shall talk of them when you sit in your house, and when you walk by the way, and when you lie down, and when you rise.
Deuteronomy 6:6-7

Train up a child in the way he should go; even when he is old he will not depart from it.
Proverbs 22:6

Fathers, do not exasperate your children; instead, bring them up in the training and instruction of the Lord.
Ephesians 6:4

Fathers, do not embitter your children, or they will become discouraged.
Colossians 3:21

Discipline them

Discipline your son, and he will give peace; he will bring delight to your soul.
Proverbs 29:17

The rod of correction imparts wisdom; but a child left to himself disgraces his mother.
Proverbs 29:15

Provide for them

Now I am ready to visit you for the third time, and I will not be a burden to you because what I want is not your possessions but you. After all, children should not have to save up for their parents, but parents for their children.
2 Corinthians 12:14

Set an example for them

For I have chosen him, so that he will direct his children and his household after him to keep the way of the Lord by doing what is right and just, so that the Lord will bring about for Abraham what he was promised him.
Genesis 18:19

Older men are to be temperate, dignified, sensible, sound in faith, in love, in perseverance. Older women likewise are to be reverent in their behavior, not malicious gossips nor enslaved to much wine, teaching what is good, so that they may encourage the young women to love their husbands, to love their children, to be sensible, pure, workers at home, kind, being subject to their own husbands, so that the word of God will not be dishonored.
Titus 2:2-5

> *As a mother comforts her child, so I will comfort you.*
> Isaiah 66:13

> *As a father has compassion on his children, so the Lord has compassion on those who fear him.*
> Psalms 103:13

With anything, and especially visible with a plant seed, when it is neglected or not responded to appropriately, it will suffer or die. The Lord intended for parents to treat their children, His children, with patience, compassion, and love, behave in ways that are in the child's best interest – and to discipline them when necessary.

We must reclaim our role as nurturers and providers. The mandate is being issued to everyone that has a child, has influence over a child or is thinking of having a child to commit to the role of a farmer. The time has come to take on the role literally – even if it takes purchasing overalls and making them the daily dress. At the crack of dawn our duty begins; praying, speaking life and making plans. What may appear to be an impossible feat, know that with God all things are possible[6].

As the farmer - the parent - we have the right, the duty and the privilege to take claim to our children – and inspire them to be great. This book will provide the blueprint, which includes both the instruction and practical perspectives to do so.

---

[6] The Holy Bible, Matthew 19:26

PART TWO:

The Blueprints

CHAPTER 4
THE LEGEND

The essentials of this book stem from an understanding of several agricultural terms. Most of these terms are common in our standard vernacular, while others are more learned in nature. To fully comprehend the blueprint of this book, learning these terms will be critical. With each term, there is added learning that will require a shift in our cognizant thinking and worldly understanding to fully grasp the base concepts of this book.

The concepts discussed in the forthcoming chapters will need to be viewed thru a filtered, wide-scope, spiritual lens. Societal ideals on parenting will need to be isolated to allow for sincere curiosity and flawless awareness of the newly introduced philosophy. Starting from a place of pure farming and overlaying modern conversations on parenting, creates a unique parallel that warrants some well-paced study and review.

Thus, the interchanging archetypes of this book, begin with a list of relevant vocabulary – defining each from an agricultural (ie. pure farming) and practical (ie. applied parenting) perspective.

Term	Agricultural Definition	Practical Perspective
Land / Soil	the upper layer of earth in which plants grow, foundation	the world; selected home for planting; womb of implementation; or spiritual grounding
Field	an area of open land, especially one planted with crops or pasture	the world; selected home for planting; womb of implementation

Cultivate	the breaking up of soil in preparation for sowing or planting	personal preparation; the process of trying to acquire or develop oneself, a quality or a skill in advance of starting a new growth experience or new/changing circumstance
Sow	the act of planting a seed in the soil with intention for it to grow	the intention, purpose and actual steps taken to produce or reproduce something new
Seed	the deposit or planting source for reproduction	an article of conception; future children or offspring; a belief, objective purpose or thought that requires manifestation to be; God's word
Reap / Harvest	the gathering up of produced fruit or crops; the benefit as a result of sowing seeds	a reflective outcome stemming from prior intent, preparation and maturation; return on your investment
Fruit	the product formed from a planted seed	children or offspring; manifested belief, thought or action
Crop	collection of fruit	collective group of children or offspring
Germination	the development of a plant from a seed or spore after a period of dormancy	the process of something coming into existence and developing after planted
Weeds	a wild plant growing where it is not wanted and in competition with cultivated plants	people/things of evil or harmful intent; interruption to productivity and growth; bad influence

Because these terms will be used frequently throughout this book, it is recommended that they be studied until the practical interpretations are clear and the analogous perspectives become second nature. Having a strong comfort level before moving forward to the next phase of this book is highly recommended so that key philosophies can be more quickly accepted and adhered to.

As a help, test your knowledge with the **Legend Exercise** provided and repeat it as many times as you need to. This exercise is also included in the Appendix, along with the correct responses.

Legend Exercise

Answer	Agricultural Term	Scenario – Physical Interpretation
	Land / Soil	A. My children, collectively
	Field	B. I made every effort to surround myself with positive influences, learn as much as possible about self-care and save money before I had my first child.
	Cultivate	C. My spouse has such strong values and those values are being passed down to our children.
	Sow	D. We purposely choose the community where we live based on the surrounding atmosphere, general spirit of the neighborhood and progressiveness of the people around us.
	Seed	E. It is a wonder and joyful moment to see my baby growing in my womb.
	Reap / Harvest	F. My child
	Fruit	G. I'm always watchful of the company my children keep; making sure that they are not bad influences or leading them astray.
	Crop	H. I'm careful about what I say to my son because I want to make sure that what he hears from me becomes a part of who he is and manifests into something positive and great when he becomes an adult.
	Germination	I. Now as adults, my children are very loving and kind; which reflects everything they were taught.
	Weeds	J. My children have all matured to be strong, loving and productive people, who give back graciously to their community.

Now that you have confirmed your understanding of the farming language and reached a level of assuredness with the parallel practical interpretations, comprehension of the formal blueprint for the farming-parent landscape will be much easier. This blueprint is the pivotal precept to understanding the overall purpose and intent for planting and harvesting a seed. It is important to build our structure on these formative principles, as they will consistently become the reminder and reflection of what we should be doing as a fruit bearer, farmer, and parent. Adding that it also serves as confirmation of the reward or consequence due in response to our labor.

CHAPTER 5
THE FARMING PLAN

God said, "Let the land produce vegetation – seed-bearing plants and trees on the land that bear fruit with seed in it. These seeds will then produce the kinds of plants and trees from which they came."
And it was so.
Genesis 1:11

From this scripture, a generational purpose and plan is established. It was not the intent to plant once and reap once. The ability to continually reproduce, by way of one seed-producing plant producing another seed-producing plant, was the very clear mandate. This continual behavior offers lifetime promise to the land and to the earth, while additionally portraying a selfless act of fervent giving.

The second notable finding in this passage is that the *obvious* was stated. "These seeds will then produce the kinds of plants and trees from which they came" or in other words, the original seed is destined to produce fruit of its likeness. An orange produces an orange and a pear produces a pear. Though some may see this 'likeness' extended only to the physical, science and reality have proven otherwise. Not only will an orange look like it's bearing fruit, but it will taste the same, require the same preservation treatment to survive and offer the same health benefits to those that consume it. Thus, everything of the bearer transcends to the new seed.

The bible tells us that we humans are created in the likeness of our Father in heaven[7]. This truth gives us all hope and assuredness that even in our imperfection, we can call and rely upon our Heavenly Father to

---
[7] The Holy Bible, Genesis 1:27

improve us and our fruit. Simply connecting with His greatness, gives us the greatest potential of all.

Call to Action
"Write the vision; make it plain so you can easily read it."
Habakkuk 2:2

"Where there is no vision, the people perish".
Proverbs 29:18

Though there is a call for Land to produce vegetation, the expectation is that before the first seed is planted, a vision be established and eventually scribed. What type of fruit do you want to harvest? How much fruit do you want to produce? Do you have the time to dedicate to proper growth of the crop? Do you have the tools and support needed to produce a good harvest? Are you prepared to take on the responsibility of producing a harvest? Have you reviewed the lessons from previous farming experiences to determine the best path forward?

These agricultural-based questions can all easily be the same preparation and planning criteria for an expectant parent. In many instances, there was no thought – and definitely no formal planning – put into the when's, how's, can's or what's regarding the birth and life of a child. Often times, it just happens and planning turns into momentary or immediate, thought-less decision making. Improving on just this simple activity would make the biggest difference in the plight of the farming parent and ultimate state of our seed.

The Promise

"Land that drinks in the rain often falling on it and that produces a crop useful to those for whom it is farmed receives the blessing of God."
Hebrews 6:7

Though the planning and vision-capturing are key to having a positive head-start, regular nourishment is the essential measure to ensure growth and good harvesting. In the above scripture, *rain falling on a seed-planted fields* can be interpreted, from a parenting stance, as the act of continuous supply of sustenance to our children, in and out of the womb. This nourishment includes both the teachings of the Good News, as well as the constant parental expressions of care and concern. Together these factors bring forth ripened harvest – and in return for this completed responsibility are God's favorable rewards.

The spiritual teachings impressed upon our seed not only bring lifelong reward to the child, but also reciprocal honor to the parent. The wisdom and experience-based teachings will prove effective in the growth of the child and parent – as individuals and as a family unit. Furthermore, these teachings never stop. At times noting that the teachings may be reactive to a current situation or proactive based on parental discernment or foresight about an impending event. Consequently, we can never hold back or defer sustenance. Doing so could be a matter of life or death.

The Consequence

"Every tree therefore that does not bear good fruit is cut down and thrown into the fire."
Luke 3:9

As a result of all life's choices and behaviors, there is also a consequence in response to our execution on the calling. Should we choose to ignore the call or pursue a different path to harvesting, there is a price to pay. In the verse, the condemnation of any tree that does not reap good fruit will cease to exist and have no further opportunity to try again. This may appear extreme, but it is a vivid indicator of how important the original decision to plant and become a farmer should be. Though the act of planting or birthing a child are uncomplicated, the *everything after* is quite the contrary.

Farming land for harvest requires preparation. To simply select a random spot in your yard, dig a hole, place in a seed and expect a mature vegetable or crop plant to produce is *hopefulness* personified. Good fruit is first the reflection of the tree in which it is was born of - and then, a product of the subsequent, ongoing and profound cultivation and nurturing invested.

As the foundational principle stated, the call was to reproduce for the purpose of reproducing. With this then, some thought should be given to what may come from a terminated reproduction - especially when there is no life-threatening condition present or the implanted state was not the result of a sexual assault of sorts. Reckless living and poor choices that disregard the *call,* do lead to spiritual consequences and oftentimes they are manifested emotionally and physically. Hence, the value of a seed is rightly matched by extreme repercussions; especially when it's life is not fully protected and there is a lack in accountability for the state of things as they are.

The next chapters are dedicated to defining this accountability. Part II of this book is a detailed, step by step teaching on the farming process for a seed, with direct correlation to the principles of parenting. The hope is that the transformation of the mind has begun and you have started to connect your parenting experience with the purpose, mission and focus of an agriculturist.

Though we have lived everyday as an individual – with our own personal destinies, plans, dreams and aspirations – we must recognize that once we birth a child, our individualism becomes the greatest sacrifice. As a farmer, our life becomes committed to raising a living organism. Likewise, as a parent, our life becomes dedicated to the upbringing of an individual that then has a sole purpose to give of itself, feed and nurture others.

CONSIDER

If the intent of reproduction actualized as it is written, no one would ever be hungry or go in need. We are all created to take care of and serve each other. Thus, conversations about poverty, joblessness, homelessness or even loneliness, would be based on imagination and not fact.

This sense of concern, love and positivity however, can't originate from *nothingness*. **Goodness** comes from **wholeness**. Thus, past understandings have been all wrong. We thought we had to receive to survive; when all the while, *we've only suffered or experienced lack because we had a deficit in giving.*

PART THREE
The Field Guide for Parenting

Thus far, we have gained a perspective of the current state of things and been introduced to the original plan and purpose for the valiant role of being a farming-parent. The next chapters are outlined chronologically through the seed-bearing process, taking patient steps through explaining both the physical plant process from the viewpoint of a farmer and then the relatable experience of a human reproducing and parenting experience.

Though the farming perspective may seem daunting, it is important to have regard for its notable semblance in the spectrum of creation. It is absolute amazement how all life, despite the source or type, *births* from a place of union, *matures* through a phase of cultivation and nourishment, and *survives* only in the face of abundant and consistent care and love. The concepts learned about a plant seed, will enhance understanding and further bring purpose to the parenting experience.

The Field Guide for Parenting provides basic facts for pre- and post-parenting situations. The concepts referenced are most effective when initiated from the beginning. Unfortunately, for many, we are well past the starting phase and are seeking reactive measures to solve current conditions. With that in mind, the path forward should include a study of all concepts, with the most immediate attention and response being particular to your actual place of alarm.

Whether you are in *a single-soon-to-be-dating* state, an unhealthy co-parenting or *divorced with children to single parenting* state, there is hope and a destination of greatness awaiting **you**, **your seed** and the **generations to come**.

*Resources for additional Farming Inspiration are located in the Appendix.

CHAPTER 6

CULTIVATION AND FERTILIZATION:
Farming Perspective

Cultivation is defined as the act of caring for or raising plants (or plant seeds).[8] Cultivating is an age-old gardening principal that is done without much thought for seasoned farmers. Experienced farmers take the time to break up or remove weeds, loosen, water and nourish soil prior to planting because they understand the necessity and risks associated when not done. Alternatively, newer or less devoted farmers may mistakenly assume that they can cut corners and achieve the same results by way of an easy or simplified process. In time, they discover how much work is really involved – or perhaps they just become complacent with the results and accept things as they are.

When committing to the role, a farmer has inherently made an agreement with himself, the fields, his budget, his time, and those depending on him that when he plants his seed, he will be dedicated and indebted to fully producing a ripe, good crop. The committed farmer is also promising to embrace the cold and the heat; and adjust himself, his behaviors, practices, and unfounded beliefs to ensure nothing disturbs the growth, development and prosperity of his seed.

To begin the multi-part cultivation process, and prepare for eventual seed planting, the farmer must first *obtain and secure a planting ground*. Selecting land for planting is a serious matter. There are many elements of the land that need to be analyzed and confirmed before making a final decision. How the land looks or merely the fact that all the right elements appear to be present does not constitute good planting ground.

---

[8] Vocabulary.com, accessed March 12, 2018.
https://www.vocabulary.com/dictionary/cultivation

Land Selection

Once the land selection process commences, there should also be an intent to purchase and secure complete ownership. For added protection and freedom to make decisions about the land, it is highly recommended the land not be shared or haphazardly engaged for a season. Sharing land or contracting it for short stay does not provide any long-term security and introduces multiple, complex issues with crop planning, harvest division and other related matters.

In good faith, the farmer is venturing to find viable, fertile land, as the health and strength of a plant will be determined by the condition of the soil. The better the soil, the healthier and stronger the plant. Better is calculated by many factors, but to start soil should not be too sandy or too hard, and it must supply the right nutrients for the plant to grow strong.

Specifically, the factors to consider when selecting land include,

Availability of water
The planted seed will require large quantities of water for sustainable growth. Thus, the water supply should be continuously and conveniently available and of good quality.

Soil quality
There are many varieties of soil and there is the ability for a seed to survive in any. However, it is very important to determine what is best for the seed type, relative to the long-term projection of what type harvest is being sought. The optimal condition of the soil desired must have the ability to maintain water retention capacity and accommodate proper drainage to avoid overflow or soggy conditions.

Additionally, the soil quality should be evaluated for its nutrient content to determine the need for any correcting measures to improve it. Ultimately, the farmer will not want to settle on the selection and depend on what it may become. The goal is to secure the healthiest field, which in turn will produce the healthiest crop.

Soil depth
Over time, the planted seed matures thru the soil and grows tall, which in turn makes it heavy – especially once it begins to bear its own fruit. Therefore, the plant will need sufficient room for proper root development to support itself. It's very important that shallow soil not be selected. Soil that does not have any depth or room for water storage tends to be easily impacted by unpredictable weather conditions.

In addition to the importance of root development, the depth of the soil additionally affects potential draining and leakage. Neither of these are optional for a healthy crop, as maintaining moisture is vital.

Soil Preparation
Once evaluation is complete, the actual preparation of the field can take place. This too, is a multi-step process that must be done before planting a seed. It can be seen throughout these processes that the planning and activities prior-to have great influence on the growth and development of the crop; ultimately determining whether there will be a harvest or not.

Nature and the world surrounding impacts the health and viability of the soil. Cultivating breaks thru the unprepared soil and allows it to breathe, receive its proper nutrition and absorb water down into the roots.

Weeds
While cultivating provides great benefit to the soil, it also dually exposes weed seeds to the surface where they can eventually die and be removed

from inhabiting the space intended for the plant to grow. Weeds are constantly growing and attempting to compete for water and nutrients. Thus, cultivating is key to interrupting the growth of weed seeds as a measure of soil protection and preservation.

Not managing weeds properly can hugely alter the farming plan. Consequently, it is extremely important the farmer has a comprehensive and ongoing task item to understand the following,

- the make-up of the problematic weed,
- what he/she may be doing to encourage the weed growth,
- where the weed is coming from and where it is showing up in your field, and
- how to get rid of the weed.

As if additional reasoning is needed, cultivating improves moisture penetration which is necessary for water retention. As more water is retained the need to have additional watering sources is decreased. Cultivating should and cannot be avoided, as it has many great benefits. In the end, the benefits will also be visually apparent because cultivated soil will be beautiful and appear renewed.

Field Preparation Steps
Once field analysis is complete and there is confidence in the selection, acquiring the land will be necessary to begin any physical modifications to it. Assuming the farmer has followed the proper steps to become the owner, the initial groundwork can begin.

Step 1: Physical field preparation
This inaugural step acts as a prelude to the more active preparatory stage. In this early phase, a farmer is both taking the first pass at viewing the exposed land, identifying the immediate clean-up required and

calculating the time, labor and financial investment necessary to achieve desired results. If the farmer remains mindful of the return they hope to receive, the amount of commitment to be expended should be well dictated.

The initial preparatory activities can include:

- bush clearing
- removal of stones, rocks and debris
- ripping – loosening of hard layers of soil which helps to increase soil drainage by opening up the soil and allowing water to infiltrate at a faster rate. This helps reduce erosion by getting the water away quicker.
- levelling of the soil

After concluding the physical field preparations, the farmer can then proceed to the activities below, which will not be detailed to avoid getting too technical. The intent is to further stress that the selection process should not be taken lightly and time should be invested to properly prepare the land for planting.

Other considerations and activities included in the soil preparation process are,

- Irrigation system installation (if needed)
- Instill soil improvements or enhancements
- Till the soil
- Tilling is another method of soil preparation that is really a more aggressive form of cultivation. In some cases, it is necessary, though this farming principal has been challenged over the last century and is often a skipped step as long as the previous cultivation steps are followed closely.

Step 2: Prepare and dig the hole

The actual digging of the hole is one of the last actions before planting takes place, but it is not the final preparation for the planting operation itself. While planting seems to be an effortless to-do, there are a few factors to be considered. They include,

Hole size
Make sure there is plenty room for loose soil in the bottom of the hole, so roots thrive.

Soil conditions
The soil conditions must be appropriate for what you are planting; which includes drainage and water and air availability

At this point, fertilizers and other organic materials can be worked into the soil to secure the strong, effective growth of the seed. Provided this is required, appropriate time should be taken to ensure all things are suitable and ready for the impending planting.

CULTIVATION AND FERTILIZATION:
Practical Perspective

Having now been taught the steps of obtaining, evaluating, securing and preparing land for planting and the applied method of cultivation from the perspective of a farmer, let's explore these same principles as they relate to the parenting experience.

The Decision

In an optimal state, becoming a parent would begin from a conscious choice and well thought out plan. Having a thorough understanding of the responsibilities, commitments and challenges of parenthood should be a formal prerequisite to having a child. Though having this full awareness does not change the activity of what's to come, it does provide a stable reference and controlled response to situations that arise. It is certainly easier to respond to a house fire when you've previously participated in a mental or actual fire drill.

Mate Selection

At some point an impulse to pursue a mate emerges and hormones and visual acuity lead the way to *picking*. As we've learned from the farmer, selecting land is more a job to be consumed by our minds. Mate selection, especially when there is likelihood or intent to produce offspring, is serious business. Choosing land, or a mate, that looks good but does not demonstrate evidence of fruitfulness, would be a disadvantaged situation. Thus, in the same manner of duty and commitment of a farmer, individuals must be extremely prudent in choosing fit ground to plant and grow their seed and crop.

The world is overwhelmed with fields of land, so much so that people have become too indolent in the choosing process and settle for the first field of land they find or the field that requires little work or investment to obtain. In either case, we are acknowledging that any potential seed planted in this field will succumb to whatever comes or doesn't come from the inconsequential nature of the entire farming plan. That alone isn't fair; and more importantly speaks contrary to God's call and the level of greatness we are seeking to inspire.

Assuming one is fully informed and sincere in their mate selection efforts, it would be expected that the end goal as much as the immediate are fully in mind. The moment eventually comes when the search is narrowed and informal selection of a companion is near. Early on, you may notice things that are glaringly wrong with your selection (eg. heavy drinker, use of extreme profanity, married, criminal behavior, clear and directly opposing beliefs, etc.), and in those circumstances, it would certainly be wise to conclude that this may not be a good investment.

However, if you observe some unalarming characteristics or behaviors that cause some pause, there is potential to categorize these pre-cultivating hang-ups as things to work past on the way to a healthy relationship. These things aren't found to be a direct reflection of the true quality and depth of your new mate, but they are windows into the eventual long-term relationship and child preparation process.

Beyond the superficial, you simultaneously should have understanding of your potential mate's ability to (1) provide support and continuously replenish oneself, (2) thrive in all seasons, and (3) grow, be consistent and long-standing. To explore each of these areas, it will be necessary to ask questions, carefully discern and purposefully listen. These areas will additionally need to be explored not just from a personal standpoint, but expand to the financial, social, professional, physical and spiritual perspectives as well. When you are selecting your mate – everything about them matters.

Though it is possible to produce a healthy, balanced, great child from a relationship that does not meet 100% of the preferred criterion, it is not the most ideal plan. The key is to not proceed with having a child until these matters are identified and addressed, which in turn allows for proactive success.

Mate Evaluation and Relationship Cultivation
To identify and address what is and what should be, many couples would find completing a formal checklist to be invasive and potentially a turnoff in finding a mate; and therefore, would dare not initiate the conversation. By taking this stance, the couple is agreeing to a union built on assumptions, hopes, unknowns and a host of unpredictables. This is a recipe for disaster and to some degree a very selfish approach to assuring a great seed, let alone a generation of greatness.

Alternatively, completing a checklist or having answers to all questions and concerns does not guarantee an issue-free relationship. It does, however, lay a framework built on known areas that you chose to either ignore, compromise on or work thru over time – which each still provides a more agreeing and collaborative approach to address and resolve issues as they arise. In all, it cannot be emphasized enough the grave importance of taking the time to know your mate.

Invoking today's reality, and calling attention to the varying statuses of relationships, the process of mate selection, cultivation and fertilization will need to be explored from 3 different perspectives. These perspectives are, (1) an individual in the selection process in hopes of having a child, (2) an individual complete with selection and is currently expecting a child and (3) an individual complete with selection and already has a child(ren) with their mate.

In the latter 2 perspectives where the selection process has already been completed, there are still important learnings, evaluation tactics and corrective measures available. The decisions, timing and sense of urgency differ for each; and a discussion will be provided for them respectfully.

Perspective #1: Individual in the selection process in hopes of having a child.

When you have not yet planted a seed or birthed a child, you are perfectly positioned to get it right the first time. The absolute best position to be in is to have an opportunity to plan, gain understanding and have a day one foundation for yourself, your mate and your child - and their eventual greatness. Though there may be a strong desire or at times an age-clock ticking, the reward is so much greater when fostering a high degree of thoroughness and patience.

To gauge your readiness and commitment (ie. duty), ask yourself the following questions.

- Do I have room in my life to take on the demands of parenting?
- Have I achieved balance with my mate, career, personal aspirations, spiritual life and time with family/friends?
- Am I emotionally ready to be fully responsible for another life besides my own?
- Have I responded to and gained relief from the Indirect Affects (ie. parental behavioral contributing to Direct Effects) and made positive to any Direct Effects (ie. consequential behaviors, feelings and emotions resulting from Indirect Affects) in *Chapter 2: The Plight of the Farmer?*

- Do I consider myself to be flexible, open-minded and willing to learn and adapt to things I've never done or not done well?

An affirmative response to the above questions is ideal, and typically recommended to be confirmed before having an expectation for your mate. It is always best to have surety with your own behaviors, desires and positions before holding someone else accountable for the same.

Proceeding thru to a thorough vetting of your mate is next in line, and hopefully among the many considerations, you have factored in a formal marriage commitment. Though some do not believe in the sanctity of marriage and are quite content with having children out of wedlock, these questions should be addressed in either state.

To now gauge the thoroughness of your current selection process, ask yourself the following questions.

- How well do I know your mate?
- How would I characterize the current state of my mate's parenting affairs? (ie. Take note of the condition of his/her fruit and past/current harvesting processes)
- How would I characterize the current state of my mate's personal and professional affairs? (ie. Review his/her fruit, past/current harvest)
- How would I characterize the current state of my mate's spiritual (not religious) affairs? (ie. Review their grounding. How do they handle stress? What gives them hope? How do they respond when the wind blows a little harder and unexpectedly? Do they exhibit kindness, and the other fruits of the spirit?) Would you rate their capacity to be strong low, and even so in those cases, how do they move forward when in this state?
- Have would I evaluate my mates 'love meter'? Can they love

thru trials? Can they love when wronged? Do they go beyond speaking love to showing it? Do they recall and keep record of your mistakes and wrong doing? Do they forgive and seek to understand, more than seek to be right?

- What is my mate's recipe for success and happiness? Is it determined by how much money is on hand or how known I am (or they are)? Do they know their purpose and how it impacts the life of others?

Responding to these questions is the same as determining the depth and quality of their soil, and also the availability and sustainability of the person's water supply (ie. support, faith and commitment). As a general principle, a person who does not fare well in several of the evaluated areas, but has a strong, consistent spiritual walk, is highly likely and very capable of growing positively in the days, weeks and months ahead. By initiating and maintaining a healthy spiritual life together, keeping it prioritized and centered, and grow in collective faith, you immediately cover your future relationship and family with extra assurance. You are more likely to weather storms, mature past problems and sustain in dry areas that can't be self-resolved, simply by abiding in divine care and order.

All things considered and your mate selection proves fruitful, your farming process is in good standing to make the last few preparations for seed planting. Keep in mind, along the way in this journey and in all life's experience, constantly managing interference and interruption will be a full-time job. It never fails, when things are going well, trouble comes knocking on the door. Whether it is your finances, friends who don't have your best interest at heart, or even family members that just can't support or accept you moving on – you should recognize these things for what they are. Like the farmer, you must understand the make-up and root of exposed weed, acknowledge your role in the existence of the weed, and have a plan to get rid of the weed. Each of these situations is taking up space, and on the path to greatness there is no room for interruption.

Final Preparations

You've made your mate selection and performed all the necessary checks and balances to affirm your choice; and additionally, gone the extra mile to remove the dead weight and destructive baggage intended to bring harm to your relationship. You are now ready to perform the final steps before the seed planting begins. This next step may appear to be more like the same, but you can never be *too prepared*. The difference at this phase is that instead of being focused on the immediate investment, benefits and return – you will need to begin thinking long-term. What may appear sufficient for a brief interaction, may not be adequate for the forever.

Thus, more active and aggressive change should be introduced; whether it is formal counseling, complete repentance and/or a spiritual revival. The more prepared you and your mate are for parenting, the more benefits to be reaped upon having a child. The preparations expand even to the final step of digging the hole. This closing phase encompasses the added essentials needed for your future child and your relationship to expand, grow and flourish. These essentials can include, purchasing and preparing the home and securing finances and savings. Making provisions for the new arrival should begin long before the seed is planted; which allows for lower stress levels and the building of reserves for the expected and unexpected.

In all, it cannot be emphasized enough the importance of taking time to evaluate and diligently select your mate and taking additional steps to cultivate the relationship *before* planting a seed. The time investment made on the front end will prove extremely worthwhile during and after the harvest.

Perspective #2: Individual complete with selection and is currently expecting a child

In this situation, we have surpassed the many steps in the mate selection process and relationship cultivation phase and it is very possible some key findings have been missed or overlooked; or are completely unknown. Considering this, and the fact that there is a child already on the way, it is recommended that both expecting parents perform an immediate assessment of the present state. It's possible that the assessment can offer quick insight and make a positive difference in the already-made family.

To assist in the assessment process, a Cultivation Audit (CA) is provided. This audit is derived directly from the questions posed in Perspective #1. This exercise will level set where you and your mate are; which may or may not come as a surprise. More importantly, by taking the Cultivation Audit, you and your mate will have a very clear picture of your relationship gaps and have the necessary information to develop an immediate remediation and path-forward plan.

After completing the Cultivation Audit, review the results summary based on your responses. As you review the summary, it is very important that there be a sense of urgency in responding to your gaps. With the new awareness, it should be easier to institute an intervention and resolve the issues more quickly – ultimately increasing the chances of a healthy harvest.

This exercise is also included in the Appendix, along with a results scoring card.

Cultivation Audit

The statements below in the **Self** section should be answered **from your perspective**, about **YOU**, as things are TODAY. You will respond using a scale of 0-5 for the selected response. A sample entry is shown, S0.

0=No opinion, **1**=Totally Agree, **2**=Moderately Agree, **3**=Neutral, **4**=Moderately Disagree, **5**=Totally Disagree

		Totally Agree	Moderately Agree	Neutral	Moderately Disagree	Totally Disagree	No Opinion / NA
SELF							
S0	*I plan to respond to this Self-Assessment honestly.*	5					
S1	I have room in my life to take on the demands of parenting.						
S2	I have a solid relationship with my mate.						
S3	I have achieved balance with my career to soon take on the full responsibility of parenting.						
S4	I am comfortable with how much I've achieved toward my personal aspirations and current life goals.						
S5	My spiritual foundation is solid and I have a stable grasp on my purpose, gifts and talents.						
S6	I have achieved balance with family/friends and defined a fair expectation on how much time I can commit to them once becoming a parent.						
S7	I am emotionally ready to responsible for a child.						
S8	I have named and responded to my Indirect Affects as mentioned in Chapter 2.						
S9	I am confident in my selection process for a mate.						
S10	I have analyzed and cultivated appropriately.						
S11	I am a flexible, open-minded person with a willingness to learn and adapt to things I've never done before or not done well.						
	SELF SECTION TOTAL						

The statements in the **Mate** section should be answered from **your perspective**, about **YOUR MATE**, as things are TODAY. You will respond using a scale of 0-5 for the selected response. A sample entry is shown, M0.

0=No opinion, 1=Totally Agree, 2=Moderately Agree, 3=Neutral, 4=Moderately Disagree, 5=Totally Disagree

		Totally Agree	Moderately Agree	Neutral	Moderately Disagree	Totally Disagree	No Opinion / NA
MATE							
M0	*I plan to respond to this Self-Assessment honestly.*		4				
M1	I know my mate well.						
M2	It is evident that my mate has produced good fruit relative to their own children and/or children they have influence over.						
M3	It is evident that my mate has produced good fruit relative to their personal affairs.						
M4	It is evident that my mate has produced good fruit relative to their professional affairs.						
M5	It is evident that my mate has a solid spiritual foundation and healthy fear and reverence for God.						
M6	It is evident that my mate is able to handle stressful or unpredictable situations well because of their spiritual foundation.						
M7	My mate lives in a state of positivity and hopefulness because of their spiritual foundation.						
M8	My mate lives out unconditional love and is able to love thru the tough times.						
M9	My mate has demonstrated that he/she can love someone that has wronged them.						
M10	My mate is able to show love, as well as speak it.						
M11	My mate does not keep record or rehash wrong doings.						
M12	My mate has demonstrated their ability to forgive and seek to understand, rather than seek to be right.						

M13	We have committed ourselves to parenting a child by all means necessary.						
M14	My mate and I have a recipe for success and happiness that is based on knowing our purpose, executing with our gifts and talents, and ultimately surviving off what we give to others - in hopes of improving their lives.						
M15	My mate and I stand firm on all decisions we've made to date.						
	MATE SECTION						
	CULTIVATION AUDIT TOTAL						

In both the **SELF** and **MATE** sections, calculate the total for each column response and record the value in the *gray box at the bottom*. Next, for both the SELF and MATE sections add the column responses across and enter the total value in the *white box*.

Then, to calculate the final totals, surmise the SELF and MATE Section Totals from the respective gray boxes and enter them in the *white boxes* labeled *CULTIVATION AUDIT TOTAL* at the bottom.

Final Results Assessment

Based on your final calculation in the SELF, MATE and CULTIVATION AUDIT total *white boxes* - encircle the range each of your results fell into on the Results Total Scale below.

For example, if your "Self" total was 12, you would encircle the 12-33 range in the yellow column box below. Likewise, if your "Mate" total was 48, you will encircle the 46-75 range in the red column box below. Complete this also for your "Cultivation Audit Total" and then proceed to the Summary of Results section. A sample scoring card is included.

Results Total Score Card

Example

	Green		Yellow		Red	
	Low	High	Low	High	Low	High
Self	0	11	**12**	**33**	34	55
Mate	0	15	16	45	**46**	**75**
Total	0	26	27	78	79	130

Record your results below.

	Green		Yellow		Red	
	Low	High	Low	High	Low	High
Self	0	11	12	33	34	55
Mate	0	15	16	45	46	75
Total	0	26	27	78	79	130

Summary of Results

<u>Green Zone</u>

If all your audit results land in this zone, you are demonstrating that your selection, cultivation and fertilization was properly completed and you and your mate are on stable ground - ready for the initial stages of parenting. Because the seed is already planted, the work to be done is already in motion. In the next chapters, the added pre-harvest duties are discussed in detail. The best recommendation is to remain alert for any lurking weeds and focused on your personal responsibilities and the relationship; all with your future child and harvest in mind.

If you achieved anything other than "0" for either of the audit sections, you should acknowledge that there remain some gaps, though small, that should not be ignored. As your seed is growing, you will want to fill the gaps and not allow them to invade, influence or negatively impact the firm, fertile ground you've established thus far.

Most importantly, focus on the Self gaps first. It is much easier to invoke self-discipline upon yourself, and your demonstrating a willingness to change goes a long way with your mate. This can be very encouraging and ultimately be a win-win…WIN. Your future child will reap so many benefits from your healthy relationship, and learn from the example that you both are setting even before they are born. This greatness can only become greater in the years to come.

<u>Yellow Zone</u>

Though the yellow zone is not the most alarming place to be, there is a flag of caution and a clear indicator that there is some work to do before you can enter the green zone. It is very possible that only one section is contributing to your total score resulting in the range of yellow. Provided that is the case, it is pretty evident if the additional work needed falls with you or with your mate.

You are also encouraged to look at each response marked 3 or above, even if the overall was in the green zone. These areas should specifically be noted as areas of focus and pause. Recalling that a 3 or above represents a space of unsureness to total un-resolve, it is important to purposely follow-up on these items.

Red zone

Discovering your result total in the red zone is likely not a surprise to you or your mate if the two of you, at minimum, have been honest with each other up to this point. Alternatively, you could be in an oblivious co-existence and somehow finding ways to push past moments of strife. To some this could be seen as a healthy, best effort because you are staying together and maintaining for the sake of your child.

It is quite the contrary and the truth of the matter is, if the child were not already on the way, being in the red zone would be a place for immediate pause on both the relationship and plans to have a child. Unfortunately, with a child already in tow under this perspective, the best recourse is to remediate with extreme time-sensitivity.

Depending on the time to delivery, you will want to pursue immediate, but careful and sincere actions to improve the state of things before the child is born. It is important to not jeopardize the health of the unborn child or expectant mother by adding stress. In this zone, it is extremely likely that the child will not be arriving in the best of situations and in the immediate moments of bonding, he or she may experience or feel disconnected. This feeling can show up as being an extremely fussy, startled or disengaged child.

If it is not possible to restore the relationship to the green zone prior to the arrival of the child, you are encouraged to escalate and entwine the necessary fixes into your daily living. Regular, intentional progress can have huge benefits. It is certainly not a lost effort, but it is one that cannot be ignored. More importantly, it is key that everything experienced in this moment of evaluation, discovery and remediation be noted for future reference. If not, the probability of repeating this cycle is high.

Perspective #3: Individual complete with selection and there is already a child(ren)

Many people find themselves long past the selection process and are currently living out parenthood with little to no strategy or plan. The ability to perform the necessary evaluations and cultivating practices recommended prior to having a child is no longer an option. Often, these parent-farmers find themselves hopeless, powerless and afraid.

It's typical for these couples to be existing in a state of normalcy, which could be functional, dysfunctional or somewhere in between. The optimal question is whether the normality of life is inflicting harm to the child or children.

This perspective of cultivating takes on a totally different face because the many pre-harvest assessments and activities are behind you and the now pressing need is to immediately direct your attention to the current state of your seed for assessment of impact.

This phase of time is marked by various degrees of urgency, mixed emotions and opposing thoughts about what should be done first. Before venturing into solving the undefined dilemma it is necessary to stress that while resolution is sought, the lifelong parenting commitment to raising a child to greatness remain an active, unwavering contract. Acknowledging past failures and owning the current ramifications are the first steps toward making a difference moving forward.

It is never too late to inspire greatness. The ability to motivate and transform the thinking, feeling and being of your child can occur when doing so shifts to priority number one and the current-state evaluation and move-forward plan are executed expeditiously.

Upon evaluation, you will find that each child has differing needs and they will additionally vary in their level of receptiveness toward your remediating efforts. No different than a weltered plant, it is often an unknown whether your last-minute watering will have a positive, long lasting effect. There have been times when the plant comes back to full life and times when no added nourishment or change in treatment brings forth optimal results. Hence, it is very important to perform a careful analysis and honest assessment of your child and situation to increase the chances for restoring them back to a *path to greatness*.

When your seed is already in harvest and amongst the elements, there is a much taller order to fulfill. Not only are you faced with the need to formally re-parent thru relevant farming phases, but do so alongside the many competing factors of the current harvesting season. In other words, a child already thriving has already been exposed and influenced by the world around them. A child has more than likely adopted certain beliefs, behaviors and perspectives that align with things that may be right and things that may be quite wrong.

Thus, the valiant undertaking of evaluating where your child is, understanding the origins and source of their thinking and determining how to recover any broken places can take on a life of its own. Unfortunately, this is where many parents will realize the true extent of the cause, effect and future effort to achieve greatness.

We cannot overlook the current crop of children and place blame on them for the failures, hard and stubborn personalities, chronic or inconsistent behaviors and their negative outlook on life. These things, as we have now learned, have a high probability of being directly attributed to the lack of cultivation and nourishing they received to-date.

Remembering that a physical seed requires constant intervention to grow and ceases to mature when there is not adequate nourishment, exposure to the sun, pruning and fertilization. With this, how can we expect our children to thrive with the barest of essentials and minimal hands-on parenting?

To the contrary, why is it assumed that greatness will occur when there are elements of over-abundance and extreme parenting present. As discussed in the instructional section, under- or over- doing anything can be detrimental to a growing plant, thus striking the right balance and doing things in the logical, most efficient manner is the most optimal plan.

Cultivation and Nourishing for Today's Child

The missed opportunities during the selection process can very possibly be seen in the attitudes and behaviors of your child today. The unfavorable traits found in yourself or your mate or problem areas in your relationship, in most cases, have rooted themselves in some way to your child. Remembering that an orange produces an orange - a fruit of its same likeness[9] – there is nothing of the bearer that doesn't extend to

---
[9] The Holy Bible, Genesis 1:11

its fruit.

To address the cultivating and nourishing process of today's child, a formal exploration of children in categories based on age ranges will be necessary. Though age is not the only determinant or gauge to determine the remediation needed, it is the most encompassing; with other factors considered if need be. In a general sense, children do not always grow and develop at the same pace, but as a baseline there are some fundamental truths that can provide an effective point of reference. When necessary for your personal situation, added recommendations will be available to ensure you are able to perform a comprehensive review and develop solutions and an action plan for each age category.

Below you will find various age groups, a detailed analysis of common behaviors in this age group, remediation methods and suggestive indicators of a successful turn-around.

Age Range: 0 – 5 years

Analysis:
In this age group, children are quite impressionable and take on the behavior and mindset of what they see and hear around them. Fortunately, because of their malleable nature, you have the greatest opportunity for a quick remediation. At this age, children have not observed or been party to any particular circumstance for a long duration of time; though not disregarding how impactful some short-term affects can be.

In saying this, however, there are visual cues that some negative behaviors have taken root. Some examples may include – most in the latter years of this age range,

- Constant crying or regular outbursts of frustration
- General unpleasant mood when the natural response would be one of great enthusiasm or excitement (ie. child being sad at their own birthday party)
- Curt or snippy response when addressed
- Preference to be alone or extremely clingy

Note: Any situations with extreme circumstances should be directed to a counselor or spiritual resource immediately.

Remediation activity should include:
- Be fully present and observe your child. Understanding timing and triggers are very important.
- Take every opportunity to address the noticed behavior in a positive manner.
- Hold your child accountable for being consistent with their behaviors and understanding the effects of their behavior on others
- Be mindful of your behaviors and on every occasion model the behavior for your child. This allows your child to be a witness to how they should act and respond.

In each activity above, there was a recurring theme of *engagement*. At this age, and all ages for that matter, spending time with your child is priceless and extremely rewarding. The engaging moments could on some occasions be spent in silence, as the *togetherness* is the significant achievement. You are demonstrating to your child that the world is secondary to them and their needs come first. You want your child to see that they are important and that what matters to them, matters to you.

At this young age, the child is in a huge learning state and you will need to take every opportunity to "teach". Interestingly, from some of the most basic activities, you are doing just that.

A few examples of actual events and possible learning activities are,

- *Playing with toys or board games together*
  This activity teaches cooperation, working together, taking turns, accepting loss, being supportive, following instructions and many other valuable life-long lessons.

- *Reading a book together*
  Reading together increases and improves vocabulary, introduces the feeling of being recognized and depended on, and teaches empathy (based on the characters in the book), patience, and taking turns.

- *Singing together*
  It doesn't matter if either or both of you are vocally challenged, singing together is one of the first activities that can introduce the acceptance of imperfections. This activity also allows your child to experience the freedom to just be, appreciate the art and not feel restricted to any form of perfectionism.

- *Being silly together*
  Again, experiencing the freedom to just be goes a long way. A child witnessing their parent in such a liberating manner, gives them an appreciation of you transforming to their level. This simple moment of flexibility builds strong bonds and trust with a child that are often difficult to build in more serious situations.

As your child grows, they may not remember the specific moments of this time, but they will have a joy in their hearts that will have permanent residence. The bond these personable moments create will propel your child to being resilient in the face of trouble and turn the other way when drama ensues. Your child will have heightened preference for positive, free-spirited and kind things because you have sown a peace-filled, optimistic and caring manner of being into their lives. Your child will exist with magnetic-dominion.

Of all things discussed, it is also very important to involve your child in a good church and keep them in the company of other like-mannered children. Keeping your child actively participating in ministry provides a solid, unwavering foundation for them when they are young. Additionally, having bible study at home further develops the parent-child bond and builds a desire for healthy, positive living. As your child gets older and starts to live out the lessons learned in the teachings, the chance of survival is greater due to the solid ground in which they stand.

"Train a child in the way he should go, and when he is old he will not turn from it"
Proverbs 22:6

The Evidence things are working:
When you are investing time in your child and **inspire** them to **dream**, they can **be**. Outwardly, you will witness a happy, super engaged, playful child and you will notice that they look forward to the next time. Adding to this, they will excel with reading, have an increased vocabulary and IQ and be socially aware and empathetic toward others.

Age Range: 6 – 10 years

Analysis:

Children at this age are like smaller versions of ourselves; mini-ME's. Though not polished or cultured in any way, these children are more exposed and potentially susceptible to unapproving conduct. Considering this, there presents a need to reverse any engrained and habitual bad behavior.

This is also the age range where other factors, exclusive of age, may be impacting in various degrees. These impacts could appear to be unresolvable, but with persistent attention and focused clean-up efforts, children in this age group can be positively redirected fairly quickly.

Some examples of the behaviors observed will likely be the same as detailed for those 0-5 years of age; noting there to be a much larger vocabulary and greater degree of physical expression.

Remediation activity:
Again, like the observation and analysis performed with the 0-5-year age group, a few additional areas may need to be considered to conclude the most effective remediation. Similarly, spending quality time with your child is again quite apropos; incorporating a critical teaching component about communication and effective two-way dialogue. Children in this age group are apt to doing a lot more talking, and a lot less listening. They are no longer a sponge and tend to take on an extreme – like being an *extroverted conversationalist* or a *shy, reserved thinker*. If it is the former, it is key that you listen to what they are saying and if the latter, what they are not saying, as both are equally important.

A child should be open to discussing the events of their day, sharing what's on their mind, inquiring about things they aren't sure about and seeking advice. Should you find that your child is talking about everything except these things, or not about these things at all – an intervention is needed. Your goal is to get to a place where they are engaging with you about random nothings – just because.

Added to the above, this age group will be the first group where you will need to do a self-check and correlate the things you see in yourself that may be reflected in your child. Considering your child is talking, fully alert and fine tuning their personality, you will need to pay extra attention to what you are saying, doing and professing. This is not the time – though it never is – to become hypocritical in any of your ways. Children should never be directed to do as you say, but not as you do. That is the absolute worst teaching method to implement with your child. The job of a parent is to create space for a child to flourish, and nothing should get in the way of that. Not even you.

In totality, these things can be considered weed seeds. Remember those? They must be mowed, tilled and removed from the vicinity of your plant seed to ensure they are receiving nourishment in full; not in part.

The Evidence things are working:
As a check and balance, you can make note of the possible behaviors below. These behaviors provide confirmation that your positive seeds have taken root and blossomed.

You will notice your child,
- asking questions about important topics
- expressing themselves thoughtfully, honest and clear
- being transparent and admitting wrong or fault without being asked
- demonstrating a pure sense of morality and expect in others what they'd expect in themselves
- challenging or bringing attention to contradictory behavior they see in you
- consulting you when they discover situations that are unfair,

unsafe or unclear

Age Range: 10 – 15 years

Analysis:
In these transitional ages, children can be seen as confused and all-over-the-place, but in most cases, they actually have a destination in mind. Your child has been immersed into the world and may be contaminated by a variety of harmful factors. This contamination stands the chance of being deep rooted and disguised with a false display of confidence, sincerity, naivety or innocence. Your child has now been introduced and is living in the space of peer pressure and comparing themselves to others. This can generate feelings of jealousy, covetousness, and ultimate confusion about who they are – and in many cases, make them extremely rebellious and highly inclined to risks taking.

At this stage, a more advanced observation needs to take place. One that is both invasive and personal. Getting into their drawers, under the mattresses, in the cell phone – and mostly in their *head and hearts* – will absolutely be necessary. You can't allow your child's need for privacy (raising my eyebrow), supersede your need to know what you don't know.

Real Life Expression

In my home, there was/is no such thing as privacy for my child. The early acknowledgement of my role to ensure they become good citizens at all costs, and their role to humbly, peaceably and lovingly appreciate the co-existing relationship we were to have – for life – helped shape the expectations of space in our home. My children did not see their bedrooms, phones, backpacks as their own, but as shared assets. They knew at any time, they could become a part of a search and seizure.

> *By establishing this understanding early, executing random explorations and of course serving sentence, over time the need to have a conversation on this topic, let alone commence a search became unnecessary.*
>
> *Many who have come to know my children will tell you the amazement of witnessing them 'tell on themselves'. I can recall occasions when I would arrive home from a day's work and I would be met with a hug and a confession. As a parent, I could not have been prouder that my children saw value in telling the truth and loved and respected me enough to not make me find out, hear it from someone else or enter a battle of accuse and denial.*
>
> *My trust in my children benefited me on many occasions and allowed me to spend less time in this area of development and more in others.*

Remediation activity:

Due to the expanded degree of issues with your child at this age, in addition to all the remediation efforts discussed in the 0-5 and 6-10 age group, the most effective response is to introduce the importance of a close spiritual relationship with God. By connecting with an age appropriate bible study group through a church or community center, supplemented by at-home study, your child will start to turn the corner of seeing things through just a mortal lens. Teaching your child at this age the principles of purposeful living and that they are created for greatness is the best defense to uncontrolled behavior. Having a strong sense of self and understanding that their existence is larger than themselves, replaces their confusion with *assuredness, confidence* and *hopefulness*.

Remaining an intricate partner and role model in this learning process will prove beneficial as well. Your child will again need to see you walking the talk – which will ultimately bring focus and resolve to the complex, confusion their life was filled with.

The Evidence things are working
Due to this age group being the most sensitive and influential, having an alert and vigilant watch on their behaviors and level of consistency is key. If your spidey sense has never been in full use, now is the time. Trust your instincts and go where your heart tells you to go. The temporary angst your child will have with you is worth the greatness to be bestowed.

Some indicators of your remediation being effective are your child,
- confessing without being prompted
- being honest, even when doing so is hard
- following up and communicating clearly and respectfully
- being thoughtful and proactive, in most things
- questioning things appropriately
- seeing themselves differently than others and being ok with being an outcast
- being a leader and empowering others to do the same
- being concerned for others and wanting greatness for them as well

Age Range: 16 years and up

Analysis:
Even in silence, your child could be screaming and desperately needing help. Their struggle could be completely camouflaged by life. At this age, it's likely you don't know your child as the person they really are – and definitely as the child they are supposed and destined to be. Life has painted them with greens, blues and browns, as they have adapted to their surroundings. Not only are they contaminated, but the virus may have metastasized. The mind, heart, spirit of your child could be so

damaged that repair is a matter only for God.

At 16, and sometimes earlier, without immediate intervention, your child could be on a passenger on a freight train with only a one-way ticket. All the missed moments prior to today, are now intense and compounded into a single collage called "a mess".

In this age group, the residential factor plays a vital role in how to approach your child. Some are still living at home, while others have already journeyed off to the world of independence. In either case, you should remain fully engaged with your child, and communicating often. When something doesn't feel right when interacting with your child – something isn't right.

As parents, we try to give our children space and allow them to be adults. Especially in the young adult years, we want them to walk their own walk. Though there is nothing wrong with this, be mindful their solo walk will be extremely difficult if they were never taught or expected to before. All the experiences in the past when they should have been taught lessons, explained why, shown how or even disciplined over – now matter. The seeds not planted during the seasons of preparation and growth have now harvested into an untaught, distracted, uncaring, inconsiderate, self-absorbed and self-seeking being. This is your child. This is your 'mess'.

Real Life Expression

*Parents sometimes miss opportunities to teach. If there was nothing else I stressed in my home, everything was a **Teaching Moment**. Over the years, I have had a gazillion of these moments. These days, the phrase alone brings a still eyeroll and chuckle from my children.*

One such teaching moment that each of my children have experienced is related to when I noticed their handwriting becoming unreadable and sloppy. This usually occurred around the 3rd or 4th grade and because I'd already witnessed their better effort, I knew an intervention was needed.

I first wanted to understand what was contributing to the new display of lazy. My second point of interest was to determine whether my child understood the effects of having poor handwriting. Of course, my children similarly shared that they didn't have a reason for the drastic change in penmanship and admittedly said "I didn't think it was a big deal".

With this response, I enrolled them in "Handwriting Camp". Because each of my children have been through the course, they can attest that after writing their name and the letters of the alphabet repeatedly for days at a time, they never wrote another sloppy paper again.

Most interestingly, this camp was not seen as a punishment, but as an exercise in learning that what you put in, is what you get out. I shared with my children that if it had not impacted their grades and performance to-date, it would. If their teacher was unable to read what they wrote, it will be considered incorrect or incomplete. Thus, if you are going to take the time to write what's correct, write it in a manner that it could be read.

Though this was a minor-matter, the value is not in the size of the matter, but the depth of the meaning and message. Whether my child was faced with a tough decision or given a simple task to complete, the objective is to think about the outcome and execute accordingly. What you sow, you reap. What you give, comes back to you in return. Give greatness, greatness becomes you.

Remediation activity:

This is an age group where all the observances and response methods from the previous age groups will be necessary - but with an additional technique added to build a stronger commitment for change. This technique is called *Truth Parenting*. Truth Parenting is a remediation method built upon acts of confession – your confession. This is a very powerful technique and a deeply restoring exercise for your child and you. At this age, you have everything to lose and everything to gain. This is your opportunity to turn your "mess" (and your child's) into a "message".

Truth Parenting can find its source from the Indirect Affects in *Chapter 2: The Plight of the Farmer*. Those behaviors, moments, feelings or situations that you identified as triggers can easily find healing for you and your child by sharing it. There is so much to be learned from our messes and pains. What caused us pain, can be reinvented as power. A power that is born from the freedom of allowing it to live outside of you. The goal isn't to let it die, especially internally – you want to let it go.

From the deep reveal, your child will see you differently. They will connect with you in a way that discipline can't. Truth is a sign of strength and it radiates above, below, around and through the most impenetrable surfaces. Honesty, transparency, vulnerability could win you back the child you thought was lost. It could also change you for the better, and your better eventually leads to your - and your child's - great.

Real Life Expression

When my daughters were preparing to leave home, and go off to college, I moved into another level of cultivation. I recognized, I would not be physically present to nourish them while they were away. So, I had a need to install an irrigation system that would work from afar. I knew that they would be responsible for their own pruning, as I would not be present to witness the daily interruptions and impacting situations. I needed to plant emotional recall so they'd FEEL me when faced with a

> *similar situation.*
>
> *At this point, I refused to lose my child over my personal embarrassment or pride. I put it all on the table and shared the details of my most unhealthy experiences with dating and the compromising positions I put myself in because I wanted attention. I was not proud of these situations, but there was a strong need to express the emotional and mental damage these choices caused me.*
>
> *Sharing my weakness, wretchedness and unrighteousness made me human in my daughter's eyes. By opening doors to my soul and taking them on the trip thru my low moments, the window of current and future communication about this topic and others was opened.*
>
> *My hope was to inspire a change in their manner of thinking – which ultimately would change or set limitations to the degree of bad or costly decisions they would make.*

The Evidence things are working

If no other age group to hold your breath for, it's this one. These are the adults of today. These are the people that co-exist with other adults and are responsible for decisions and sometimes the lives of others. By way of the many remediation activities discussed, including Truth Parenting, you will want to observe the following in your child to know your interventions have been effective.

Your child will,
- live out loud and be transparent in their ways
- feel convicted and seek repentance
- have a stronger desire to please God, themselves and you
- have shorter stints on the wrong side of the tracks
- seek first to understand
- …and all the behaviors described in the previous age groups

In this age group, you will not be able to control the decisions or stop bad things from occurring. Your goal is to plant enough good seeds, continue cultivating the surrounding spaces and provide enough nourishing support for when – not if – a mistake or wrong move is made. By doing so, the journey back up will be faster and easier.

Our children should not see prison or a cemetery as their fallback plan. However, we should recognize that this *is* the plan when developing a better one was never a past reality. Added to this is whether an understanding of rewards and consequences was ever cultivated. We can't expect our children to live out a concept they were never held accountable to. Hence many parents experience unnecessary grief when they eventually the child must pay the cost for their actions.

If seeds were never sown in honesty, the child is likely not to be honest. If saying no and meaning no was never cultivated, it's likely your child will succumb to things that are not in their best interest; especially because saying yes is easier and feels better. If your child was never expected to communicate their feelings, don't expect to ever know what they really think and their true state of mind.

Be mindful that the cultivation and fertilization phase repeats itself as often as it needs to – with your mate and with your child – over the full course of your parenting years. The art of cultivation is even critical after a child is born and the "seed plant" then takes on the form of beliefs, thoughts and actions that are imbedded in the child as they grow. The hope is that the continual process of cultivation further enhances the maturity, prosperity and overall quality of life for your child. This idea will be further discussed in future chapters.

CHAPTER 7
PLANTING: Farming Perspective

Again, channeling the farmer within, we covered in *Chapter 6: Cultivation and Fertilization* the importance of selecting the best land and preparing the soil for the eventual planting of the seed. In total, the cultivation processes described are critical practices that cannot be taken lightly. If you find yourself at the planting phase and have not yet evaluated the availability of water, nor the quality or depth of the soil, it's a bit too late.

Soil is the key element required to grow plants; and not just any soil will do. Soil cannot be assessed based just on the visual appearance, but instead studied, tested and prepared to ensure its fertility and ability to produce a stable, healthy crop. It cannot be expressed enough that planting the seed without appropriate cultivation can be detrimental to proper planting, growth, harvest and even *reproduction*.

The concept of planting a seed appears simple – dig a hole, place the seed in the hole and cover the seed with soil. Unfortunately, as many farmers have discovered there are several more considerations and added complexities. One of which, and of foremost thought, is whether the timing is right. Planting a seed too early can produce weak, awkward seedlings, or they could be killed off immediately by the current, unstudied conditions. Alternatively, planting the seeds too late shortens the time to mature, which is not optimal either. To calculate the best timing, it is highly recommended that weather conditions be evaluated and preparations to plant in the spring season are made. Understanding the seasons is discussed further in *Chapter 9 – The Seasons*.

Once timing is confirmed, and all other factors remain intact, the planting process can begin.

The Planting Process

The easiest step of all processes, as well as the step that brings the farmer the most satisfaction is planting. (Umhmm... I hear you). This step brings additional excitement because it is the inaugural activity to reaping a future harvest. Steps 1 and 2 have been covered in the previous chapter, but worth noting to demonstrate the dependency of each activity along the way.

- Loosen and moisten the soil
- Dig a hole
- Plant the seed in a hole twice in depth as it's width
- Cover the seed with dirt, and gently pack it down into the soil
- Water the seeds, if necessary

After Planting

When a seed is planted it first grows roots. It is immediately connected and seeking support to further flourish and survive. The roots allow the plant to have access to more water and once they take hold, evidence of the connection eventually emerges and plant life becomes visible to others. At some point, shoots or plumules begin to grow, including the stem. The plant's leaves begin to grow outwardly and take in energy from the sun. Development continues until there is eventually living fruit. The small plant that emerges and eventually breaks through the soil has now completed the process of germination.

Though a fluid process, there is a period of time prior to germination when a seed goes into a dormant state until certain conditions are met. These conditions can be having proper amounts of water, oxygen, temperature, and light. Once met, the seed begins to expand as it takes in water and oxygen. The seed's coat breaks open and a root comes forth from the seed, which is followed by a plant shoot which contains the leaves and stem.

As with many of the other processes affecting seeds, germination can be further impacted by several things. A few things that can cause poor germination are:

- Overwatering can cause the plant to not have enough oxygen.
- Planting seeds too deeply causes them to use all their stored energy before reaching the soil surface.
- Dry conditions mean the plant doesn't have enough moisture to start the germination process and keep it going.

Caring for seeds after germination occurs is not difficult, but a multipart effort. The different components of the care plan are damping off, nutrition, temperature, water, light and transplanting. When done properly, the success of healthy, vibrant seedlings increases dramatically.

Other notable care processes are listed below.

Damping Off
After germination and the sprout begins to be exposed, there continues to be risks present. Damping off is a fungal disease that causes plants to wither and die. Damping off can stem from contaminated soil and then made worse by incorrect watering techniques. The threat can be found in seeds that were rotted before they germinated, decay, or infection at the root or soil level, all causing young plants to collapse.

To prevent or control these diseases, it is important to plant seeds in sterilize soil. External intervention, like the use of anti-fungal sprays, can be used to prevent or respond to disease. Keep in mind, however, that when these sprays are used, the germination process can be interrupted.

Nutrition
Providing supplemental food to the seed is one of the most basic requirements to growth. Though noting that feeding the newly formed plant too early can burn roots and immature foliage.

The new plants require the best care before they can be fully. This care extends beyond just providing water, supplemental nourishment is also needed to ensure proper growth and development.

Watering
As seed grow, watering will be mandatory; although the intent is to keep the soil moist and not soggy. It is important to allow the soil to somewhat dry between waterings. A farmer should have proper understanding and technique with watering, and all other steps. Doing too much or too little can prevent the seed from growing.

As the seed begins to show visibility, the nourishment requirements change and must be monitored closely.

Light (and darkness)
In addition to the watering needs, seeds also require a great deal of light to grow. As much value as the sunlight brings, darkness also has its place. During times of darkness, seedlings have an opportunity to rest. As they grow however, the amount of light required increases.

Temperature
In addition, temperature is important in the germination process. If a

seed is in an environment lacking the right temperature, its chance of success is severely limited, even if all the other elements are present.

When things aren't going right

As the seeds grow, visible signs may surface that indicate there is a problem. Discoloration, or yellowing of leaves, is a common sign an adjustment is needed in your nourishment process. It is recommended that the farmer evaluate the light intensity and adjust the periods of darkness the plant is getting. Just as too much or not enough of either can be an issue, adjusting watering and fertilizer to more appropriate levels are important.

Seeds don't necessarily need fertilizer in the early stages, but if this has already introduced into the regular nourishment routine, the farmer may want to lessen the application. Minerals from fertilizer can build up very quickly and choke the plants. If a large amount of fertilizer has already been applied and white deposits are visible around the drainage holes, an immediate need to flush the plant gradually with water and ceasing fertilizer application will be necessary. Alternatively, if fertilizer has not been applied and the plant is yellowing, administering a single application may be incentive needed.

Not every seed produces a plant and there could be many reasons why. It is recommended that the farmer thoroughly evaluate, determine what's best interest and if, and when the time is right, try planting again.

PLANTING: Practical Perspective

Up to this point, there has been an overwhelming amount of discussion about the importance of properly selecting a mate and getting prepared to welcome a new arrival. More than any other commitment or investment, having a child has its call, purpose and consequence directed from biblical verse. While planting a seed is a joyful occasion and excitement looms about the new life being created there is no going back or *un-planting*. Once a seed is planted, life forms and a soul lives.

As referenced from a farming perspective, the planting process is the easiest, shortest, most joyful activity of the entire farming plan. Planting is the initiating activity to a lifetime of duty and attention. Therefore, as with a plant seed, the matter of *time* must also be considered. Even if all things are in the green zone with you and your and positive cultivating practices are in place, introducing a child into the picture at the wrong time could change everything.

Hence, confirming your life's season (discussed *in Chapter 9: The Seasons*) can help you gauge your readiness. Even asking yourself simple questions like, 'am I comfortably enjoying my free time and space?' or 'am I established and satisfied with my status and feel open to welcoming change and interruption into my life?" can offer insight.

A recommended activity that can give you a practical indication of proper timing, is to spend time with someone else's child, preferably an infant. From this experience, you will obtain not only a response to your timing question but an opening into what life events, feelings or circumstances will pinpoint the right time. In addition to spending time with a child, having meaningful dialogue with the child's parents would be beneficial as well. You should be interested to learn about the financial and time commitments made, changes they have had to make to accommodate the new arrival, challenges they've faced due to the family addition and the impacts to their relationship and personal self.

Once timing has been confirmed, *may the planting begin.*

Proper planting

Because we know that in a farming sense, seeds require water/nourishment, proper temperature, favorable weather conditions, appropriate lighting and healthy soil to germinate, it is evident that again we have a duty to ensure that we are constantly evaluating our lives to set our seed up for success. The Indirect Affects introduced in *Chapter 2: The Plight of the Farmer* must remain balanced, if not completely resolved for your child to properly harvest.

Beyond Planting – Nourishment

In consideration for the many that are beyond establishing parenthood from a place of initial conception, *planting* and *nourishment* will need to be expanded to address the many topics relevant to this audience of parent-farmers. It is essential to both new and seasoned parents to understand the principles of the nurturing phase.

This book is intending to respond to the optimal state of parenting, as well as to today's reality - offering both inspiration and intervention. As so, the nourishment topic will be divided into two discussion segments – *Nourishment - In the Womb* and *Nourishment - In the World.*

Nourishment - In the Womb

What nourishment would be necessary to ensure our seed thrives in the womb?

While a child is developing in the womb conditions can change and issues impacting fertility, stability and the overall state of things can arise. Those things that are within our control should be managed appropriately. Whether it is diet, exercise, stress control, vitamin supplements or general prenatal care, we should make it a priority to maintain a proper womb for the child.

Water intake is one of the most critical nourishing measures required to ensure proper hydration. It must be noted, however that everything in and around the womb has an impact to the growing child. Even during the months of development, the child's ability to absorb its surroundings is a divine phenomenon. Never for a moment assume that your minor heartache or sad disposition matters *not* to your unborn child.

> **Real Life Expression**
>
> I can recall during the time of my 3Ds, I found myself down at times and often distant and recluse. As much as I exhibited great strength and pushed past the sadness, drama and disappointment, the effects of the situation showed up somewhat in the early personality traits of my youngest daughter. When she was born and thru the early years, it was tough to get a smile out of her.
>
> Though she was a happy child and exhibited a warmness towards me and close family members, she did not particularly offer the same to others. Some would even suggest that she was "grumpy or mean'. I knew and often said that my mood, my lack of eating as I should have and the nature of the many things happening around me had an impact on her – even from within the womb.
>
> Thanks to many of the principles discussed in this book, my daughter is well accomplished and socially adept. Though she continues to have a low tolerance for foolish things, she is very strong, a natural leader and exhibits a high moral compass.

When things aren't going right

In situations where nature interrupts and ends the birthing process, we are forced to make mental and emotional adjustments to reconcile the loss of the child and realize that there are things we may never understand why they happened. The long, painful healing process eventually reaches a point sometime after, and decisions commence regarding whether, and if fitting, when the process can be initiated again.

Nourishing - In the World

For today's children, proper nourishment is still an absolute requirement. Depending on the living arrangement between you and your child, the degree and type of nourishment you can provide will differ. If your child lives with you, you have the greatest opportunity to ensure they have necessary sustenance, are in and around healthy environments and are prepared for independent survival.

Alternatively, when your child lives outside of you home, providing the same level of assurance and support may be difficult. You can, however, make it a point to inquire, show concern or even provide support if you suspect there is a strong need. Providing this assistance could easily serve as a Teaching Moment for the future. See *Chapter 6: Cultivation and Fertilization* for a reminder of this concept and its benefit.

As a confirming measure, some key checkpoints to validate against are listed. If you are confident that your child would have an affirmative response for these items, there is strong probability your child has and is receiving the proper care and inspiration needed, at least in the place in time you are assessing. Hence, reconfirming every so often is a great all-consuming nourishment tool to measure your great seed by.

My child is,
- getting proper sleep
- performing well in school, extracurricular activities and/or on their job
- communicating thoughtfully and respectfully
- demonstrating the ability to lead and make logical, thought-based, good decisions
- asking questions that matter
- seeking guidance, sharing their problems and offering a solution to consider
- responding to challenges with a healthy attitude
- empathetic and demonstrating selfless acts of kindness

- saving and/or spending their funds wisely
- choosing friends wisely and playing well with others
  Noting that this is not the same as them having a large entourage of friends.
- maintaining a relationship with God and demonstrating spiritual growth
- has a desire to know their purpose or how they can bring goodness to others

If you are unable to confirm some or (hopefully not) any of these checklist items to be representative of your child, it is recommended that they become candidates for Teaching Moments or a serious, life-depending conversation where change can be inspired. You may discover that you may be the change. Recalling from previous reading, be sure you are the model for what you want to see in your child. You additionally will want to adjust your time, engagement, communication or level of transparency to afford your child every opportunity to be great.

Your child is a replication of you. Who they are genetically and otherwise, is a direct reflection of who you are. What we sometimes forget is that who they become is who they will beget. This offers reasoning for the family trees filled with broken, fragile, lack-lustered branches. Ultimately where there is no productivity or growth, there is extinction. The genes we pass along don't just determine physical characteristics, but also character.

So, for the sake of your current child and the generations to come, start with addressing your behaviors, issues and struggles. The sooner the tree is treated and restored to health, the sooner it will produce and impact good fruit.

"Either make the tree good and its fruit good, or make the tree bad and its fruit bad; for the tree is known by its fruit.
Matthew 12:33

In all cases, especially when self-driven attempts to heal have failed, tapping into the root is the best recourse. It is only from the foundation that unyielding strength, motivation, grace, mercy, and forgiveness can be rebirthed.

CHAPTER 8
HARVESTING: Farming Perspective

At some point, the labor of planting, cultivating and nourishing reaches a period when a return on the investment becomes available. This phase of time is known as harvest time. The act of harvesting is one of the most important and extremely rewarding activities on the farming calendar. Harvest marks the point in time when crops are matured and are ready to be gathered in for sale, reproduction or consumption. It is important to understand that crops should be harvested free of damage and under conditions that allow them to maintain good quality. Unbeknownst to many, the instant a crop is removed from the ground, or separated from its parent plant, it begins to deteriorate.

With this understanding the farmer must remain just as attentive and protective of their crop as they were when they planted it a season ago. Once the state of the crop is confirmed, the harvesting process can begin. The process is comprised of a variety of activities, some of which have been automated or mechanized in modern day farming. Of note, a farmer should be well informed of each activity and choose the specific combination that is appropriate for their crop.

The various harvesting activities and a brief description are listed below.

- *Reaping*
  Cutting the mature portion above ground, but leaving the roots bedded for a regrowth

- *Stacking/Piling*
  Temporarily storing the harvested crop in stacks or piles

- *Hauling*
  Moving cut crop to the threshing location

- *Threshing*
  Separating the paddy grain from the rest of cut crop. Usually requires the crop to be "beat" in order to get rid of anything that does not belong

- *Cleaning*
  Removing immature, unfilled, non-grain materials. Doing so helps the crop to dry faster, store better, reduce dockage at time of milling and improve milling effect and quality, reduce disease and improve yields when cleaning.

- *Field drying*
  Leaving the cut crop in the field and exposing it to the sun for drying

- *Bagging*
  Putting the threshed grain in bags for transport and storage

In traditional harvesting, activities such as field drying and stacking/piling are not recommended because they can lead to rapid quality deterioration and increased harvest losses – but again, the farmer would need to decide what's best for their crop.

Crop Failures and Avoiding Them

As much as the general focus and excitement is on reaping the harvest, it is important to have awareness of what potential failures could occur during this season. Harvest failure is when a crop yield is below what was expected, typically caused by the plants being damaged, killed, or destroyed, or affected in some way that they fail to form edible fruit. Crop failures can be caused by too much or too little rainfall, eventual effects of poor soil quality or even from a plant disease.

Some of the previously mentioned contributors of crop failure are nature induced, however there are a few that are controlled by the farmer. To properly harvest and protect the yield, the most critical recommendations are to perform the reaping at the right time, when the soil is at the right moisture level. Right time is broken down into two segments – phase of time and time of day.

In the case of some harvests, reaping too early would result in a larger percentage of unfilled or immature plants. Alternatively, harvesting too late leads to excessive losses and increased plant damage.
Time of day is equally important and farmers are trained to reap harvest in the cool of the day to reduce excessive moisture loss and wilting. Most crops are freshest and turgid early in the morning and harvesting in the middle of the day or when the harvest is wet should be avoided; as both can lead to spoilage.

Post-Harvest

The completion of harvesting marks the end of the growing season, or the growing cycle for a particular crop. Unfortunately, this does not end the farmers responsibility to the crop. After the original harvest, a farmer then enters a phase of time called post-harvest or harvest maintenance. During this time of harvest maintenance, a farmer is just as interested in loss or damage to their harvest as they were during the growing phase and must ensure that proper attention is paid to the cooling, cleaning, sorting and packing of the crop.

Some basic understandings of what could cause post-harvest loss and affect the maturity of the crop are listed below. The duty of the farmer is to remain cognizant of each potential risk and manage their crops accordingly. These risks can include,

- Improper harvesting
- Poor handling of the produce from the field through to the market place
- Inappropriate container and use of packaging material
- Poor storage conditions
- Poor transportation and distribution system
- Lack of adequate and appropriate storage facilities

Of note, only good quality harvest will be afforded with a long, post-harvest life.

HARVESTING: Practical Perspective

"Let us not grow weary of doing good, for in due season we will reap, if we do not give up"
Galatians 6:9

From a newborn state of being, harvesting is a brand-new event that is only new once. We typically, by way of doctor's orders know the expected due date of the baby and are afforded a trusted medical update on the readiness and condition of the child. This, however, does not reflect total ripeness. The conditions of our child, along with those around our child in-total provide the better indicator of *things are* and *things to come*.

The delivery, or time of harvest, will be a quick event in comparison to the growing time, but the high anticipation of the moment and emotional reflection make for a very intense moment. Everything that had influence on the growth of the child - positive or negative - will become visible for all to see. The physical appearance and mental state of your child will greatly be determined by the shared looks and psyche of you and your chosen mate. In like manner, the emotional well-being passed on to your child will be reflective of the experiences endured during their time in the womb.

With this being said, the investment in mate selection, cultivating, fertilizing, nourishing and harvesting – however thorough or not – will debut live on-stage the moment the baby arrives. From the moment the child exits the mother's womb, they become part of a very large ecosystem; filled with people, events, and environmental factors of influence. Everything you did or did not infuse during the time in the womb becomes vulnerable to immediate and dramatic change outside of the womb. Thus, more than being a moment to marvel over the beauty and splendor of the newborn child, the formal protective steps of the harvesting process must begin.

The day one agenda for your new harvest must include a recurring action item to observe and affect the world around them. Exposing your child to unhealthy teachings or any behavior noted in *Chapter 2: The Plight of the Farmer* as an Indirect Affect must not be tolerated – from your mate, family, friends, or even you. Therefore, constant evaluation will be required to ensure your child's environment maintains a positive, stable footing. This includes relations between you and your mate; which remains important for the duration of your child's life.

From a newborn harvest, it doesn't take very long to *bring in the crops* – unless you are one of the unfortunate, extended laborers. However, once the newborn child arrives, they enter a continual rotation of all the previous farming phases. At some point, they will eventually reach a place of another harvest, a time known as post-harvest or harvest maintenance. Upon post-harvest, another world of choices, challenges, desires, influences, needs, desires, tendencies, temptations arise. From this place, the harvesting conversation changes its tone and expresses the concepts in a manner that benefits *today's child*.

Post-Harvest: Today's Child

It would be quite reasonable for some parents to fast-forward to this chapter and section, as the relevancy of previous phases is a bit immaterial. Certainly, the learning provided in choosing a mate and cultivating our seed before this moment in time offers great reflection, it does not provide an immediate understanding of *what now* and *what next*. Like the many exercises provided in the earlier phases, even at post-harvest, the understanding you need will only come from a patient, sincere, deep chronological evaluation of your child's life. If you can pin-point the specific phase of time or event (*in plural - if fitting*) you will have a better chance in having effective recovery while you continue the active steps of the post-harvest phase.

After your child is born, your farming boots do not come off, they actually get tightened. Post-harvest is a time to tap into more unconventional farming tools. The work in bringing life to your child does not compare to the laboring required in the years to come. As of this reading, you could be knee deep in situations that appear unrecoverable and hopeless. It is this perception, that becomes the first thing to change.

> *"Those who go out weeping, carrying seed to sow, will return with songs of joy, carrying sheaves with them"*
> Psalm 126:6

Greatness is possible. With God, all things are possible[10]. Even when things are at what you would consider *the worst*, giving up on your child is not an option. Altering thoughts of despair, taking the time to understand and educate yourself, and speaking life to the situation is the starting place for improving your circumstances. If you can see past this phase, and begin to exude confidence in what's possible, it is only a matter of time before greatness becomes a stable and consistent manner of living.

In *Chapter 1: The State of our Seed*, we discussed various ages and their relative degrees of behavior. This concept could also be relevant in the harvest phase; especially considering the many contributors to post-harvest crop failure or loss. However, in this instance, the belief is that some overarching, foundational principles can offer a higher probability

---
[10] The Holy Bible, Matthew 19:26

of a productive, prosperous, long life for your child.

The most basic of these principles is instilling proper values and beliefs into your child, or immediately correcting any that have taken a detour. What we believe and what we feel affect how we behave and treat others. The morals and perspectives your child holds dear to them could be the weed that is draining the very life from them. Even at maturity, things that are planted or sown into your child become "internal seeds". These seeds, once they take root, must be cultivated and nourished, and protected from damage and destruction. These seeds will eventually harvest into a new behavior, manner of thinking, and state of being – a being of greatness!

What presents itself in the post-harvest phase is in most cases in response to how the child was taught and disciplined. If you find that you are in a repetitive cycle of the previous phases and true ripeness does not occur, it is clear sign that there is a critical outstanding learning. Getting thru situations with a half-baked approach will not work. You can't plant and not water, expecting growth - just as much as you can't water and never plant, and expect life. Hence, each phase is dependent upon each other and ultimately brings you to a phase of harvesting.

To reap a harvest or acquire the return from your labored investment, you must fully complete each of the previous phases. A crop must be ripe before removing it from the fields, just as our children should be ready to be in - *not of* - the world at any given time[11]. So, when we discover our inefficiencies along the way in the many farming phases, we must recognize that there could be delay in our harvest and they not be ready when society says they should be. Thus, we cannot take the job of a farming parent lightly.

[11] The Holy Bible, 1 John 2:15-17, John 17:16,

In parenting terms, it would not be wise to spend years cultivating, fertilizing and nourishing to then have a late-breaking, avoidable incident that causes impact to your fruit.

Knowing your child is ready for the post-harvest will require confirming the following:

- Your child has deep, grounded roots and demonstrates a level of maturity that can survive on his/her own.
- You have witnessed your child separate from the world and they are able to exist alone.
- Your child is comfortable in their own skin, happy with who they are and not seeking to be a carbon copy of someone else.
- You have induced challenging situations with your child and witnessed that they respond and react in a manner that is healthy, logical and calm.
- You have thoroughly addressed any sin or immature attributes in your child and have confidence that they are relieved of it. This step, if not done prior to harvesting, will need to be done sooner rather than later. This failure alone could cause quick destruction to your child and have immediate and irreversible consequences.
- You have exposed your child to the *son* and given them a firm grasp of the Living Word. Your child understands their responsibility in a world of sin and maintains a high road.
- Your child is set-up for success and has a reasonable grasp of his/her spiritual, social, emotional and financial plan. Your child has goals and is starting to understand their purpose.

You may have not had perfect responses to the items above, but the closer you are to affirming each, the more stability your child will have. In any area that you found there to be a void or level of uncertainty, it is worth spending extra time cultivating or staying engaged with post-harvest.

> *Real Life Expression*
>
> *When I moved away for college, I knew I would not be returning to my parent's home. Not because I hated being there, but because my wings had been properly clipped and I'd been thoroughly trained to fly. I felt very strongly that I had received proper grounding – spiritual foundation, support, love to sustain me and a place of reference when – not if – things went awry.*
>
> *I knew from the moment I left home that my parents had cultivated the world around me, planted my roots deep in biblical teachings and investing the time to instruct me on life, finances, and other key matters. Some of what I learned was directly taught, while others were learned by observing my parents with my siblings. Some takeaways grew to become things I continued with my own children and others I reconfigured in a manner that allowed for improved communication and response between myself and my child.*
>
> *In my era, asking "why" was not an option. If questioned, my parents instantaneously replied, "don't ask me why". I found this to be an interesting phenomenon considering I really wanted to know why and having that answer would've helped me to process the situation and apply the new learning to ensure a better outcome. So, without knowing "why", I of course followed my parents request, but spent a lot of personal time reflecting and somehow determining the why on my own.*
>
> *In saying this, I became a parent that offered the "why" to my children – and shared it before it was asked. My children appreciated the time and attentiveness I provided, which ultimately helped them grow to such admirable behavior because things just made sense. They understood the pros, cons, repercussions, and risks. Thus, their approach to most things was with a logical, common-sense, forward-thinking approach. Though*

> *every outcome wasn't perfect, each situation had great potential and contributed to the great afterall.*

Harvesting too late

If you are a parent that just can't let go or have your own fears that your child will not survive, you must understand that you are not behaving in the best interest of your child. God gives every individual a walk and purpose. No one, including you should intervene or interrupt God's plan. You will have to trust in your cultivating, nourishment to date and let your child go- and live. Holding on too long, can create a dependency that is problematic in the long term. Your child will need to learn how to make decisions, stand on their own and experience the ups and downs without direct intervention. That's the purpose of keeping the roots planted. No matter how far they go, they will always come home.

Train up a child in the way he should go, and when he is old he will not depart from it.
Proverbs 22:6

Alternatively, in cases where no foundation has been laid and no solid footing is in place, the future is unfairly positioned. A child in this predicament could be easily swayed and end up in precarious places. Selecting friends, finding a mate and the many other decisions they will make can be misguided.

In this instance, a bit of patience needs to be invoked, as additional time, teaching and inspiration will need to be offered to fill the gaps that exist. Many of the evaluations, practices and process steps discussed in the earlier chapters of this book may need to be used to remediate the lost opportunities during the cultivating and nourishing years. The hope is that sooner, rather than later, your child will be filled with seeds of greatness, seasoned with a little age and time.

When you raise your child in a purposeful manner, where they will be capable and equipped to live out your teachings, and then repeat for their future seed – this leads to *generational greatness*.

CHAPTER 9
THE SEASONS: Farming Perspective

As defined in the modern dictionary, a season is one of the four divisions of the year; termed spring, summer, autumn/fall and winter. Each season is marked by particular weather patterns and daylight hours, resulting from the earth's changing position with regard to the sun[12]. By even the calendar, seasons have been divided by a start and ending month and day.

From the perspective of a farmer, the weather, lighting conditions and earth's state of rotation all matter. What they should be doing and how they should be interacting with their crops are completely dependent on the time of year. Understanding this timing and the expectations of each season, make for a great harvest.

Winter - *The Planning Season*

During the winter season, temperatures are typically low and there is reduced daytime and minimal sunlight. Due to these weather conditions seeds lie dormant and metabolize at low levels. Though there is minimal growth for most seed during the winter months, it is not impossible to experience some transformation. For example, during winter dormancy, plants do conserve nutrients and will often shed, provided they have sprouted above ground.

The winter season is not lost time, as farmers use this uneventful time to plan for next year's growth. The farmers are busy reviewing the previous year's crop, assessing the successes and failures; and

---

[12] Merriam-Webster Dictionary, accessed April 3, 1018. https://www.merriam-webster.com/dictionary/season

making equipment and supply purchases to aid in the upcoming sowing season. Preparedness keeps the farmer steps ahead of the upcoming change in weather conditions and crop needs.

Spring - *The Harvesting and Maintenance season*

Once the ground has thawed out from the cold of winter, farmers move into the spring season. The season is marked by the leaves appearing on the trees, the grass growing in green, and flowers beginning to bloom. This is a busy season for farmers. In March, once the weather warms up, farmers begin to prepare the soil for planting. In April and May, the fields are planted with the seeds of crops; which also means that the farmer will have to begin the diligent efforts of protecting their new crop from interference from unwanted pests such as insects and pathogens.

Summer - *The Growing Season*

During the summer, the farmer is still busy weeding and keeping the crop clean and protected. The temperatures are a bit warmer so the increase in interference is expected. it's the farms busiest time of the year and visually the crops begin to show evidence of harvest readiness.

Fall – *The Field Preparation Season*

The fall season is typically active from late September to late December, and dedicated to the farmer getting things ready for the cold winter months. Harvesting is the big to-do and once the crops are fully ripened and dry, they can be reaped. The fall is also characterized by inconsistent weather and thus making it hard for a farmer to know the perfect timing for the many pre-winter preparations. Over time, a seasoned farmer is able to forecast and predict with improved accuracy.

THE SEASONS: Practical Perspective

For everything there is a season, and a time for every matter under heaven: a time to be born, and a time to die; a time to plant, and a time to pluck up what is planted; a time to kill, and a time to heal; a time to break down, and a time to build up; a time to weep, and a time to laugh; a time to mourn, and a time to dance; a time to cast away stones, and a time to gather stones together; a time to embrace, and a time to refrain from embracing;
Ecclesiastes 3:1-22 ESV

"He said to them, "It is not for you to know times or seasons that the Father has fixed by his own authority."
Acts 1:7 ESV

We have often characterized sowing seeds and reaping harvest as a seasonal event. Though this is true, we must understand that the seasonal concept differs between literal crop production and raising our children. As it relates to farming, seasons are defined by a distinct calendar and changes in weather condition, whereas with parenting - seasons are defined, evidenced and best understood by way of a divine connection and revelation.

According to the standard dictionary, a season is the time of year when a particular fruit, vegetable or other food is plentiful and in good condition, or *an indefinite or unspecified period of time*. Thus, interpreting the latter definition, calculating or depending on weather changes to predict when it's time to move from one phase to another or conclude that our work is done would not be the wisest.

With this new understanding, we learn to gauge seasons by the active events and ultimate purpose; and addressing the seasonal changes with proper response. At any given time, we may find ourselves in any period of time and it is very important that we have full awareness of what is expected to occur in *that* season. Knowing this, it is quite possible to be in an extended period of growth and instead of a season of harvest following, we find ourselves in another planning season. In all, we should seek to make conscious decisions and respond prudently to the occurrences and activities as they are.

For purposes of also understanding that along with our children, we experience seasonal change, the study of this topic should be done from a parenting and personal perspective.

Winter - *The Planning Season*

The winter season of life should be a time dedicated to initiating and maintaining safeguards from harmful influences, planning for growth and focusing on the eventual harvest. This season can be brutal if proper maintenance and care is not taken and all the work to-date could take unrecoverable steps backwards. The world can be cold and harsh, but staying connected to the unchanging, strong and protective hands of God, the winter season can bring great joy and reward.

Another possible benefit of this season are the quiet moments of solitude available while hibernating inside. This time can be quite valuable, as the time could be used to enhance learning and personal development (working out, changing unhealthy habits, etc.). The winter should not be time lost, but time gained in getting ahead of what's to come.

Spring - *The Harvesting and Maintenance season*

As a parent, this is the time to assist, influence and inspire productivity and development in our children. This season brings fresh, forgiving and loving renewal to anything that may have been lost, disappointing or distracting in the past. Just as our lives sometimes go on pause or takes steps backwards, our children face the same challenge. Hence, we should take this season to recall and teach principles of survival and unconditional love – how to push through adversity.

Thanks to the warming season, uncontrolled adventure and other possible interruptions present themselves without introduction. Due to this, the need to revisit some of the protections used in the winter become important again. It never fails – the closer you get to reaping harvest, the more trouble brews or comes near. Recognizing how close you are to receiving the return on your investment should provide enough fight to not turn back or give in.

Summer - *The Growing Season*

Who doesn't love summer? Even the insects get excited and make their presence known. During the summer, everything is in full bloom and wildly exposed. Thus, the protections and safeguards passively used during the winter and spring months should be escalated for more aggressive use. If there is no other time to go into full protective mode, it is in the summer.

Remembering that the seed in due harvest could be *independence, revival, renewal or birth* of your child, or even *a learning or blessing* for yourself or your child - in any of the circumstance, the cultivating and nurturing invested has matured and the moment to feel, see and be GREAT is now!

Fall - *Field Preparation Season*

This season is also known as harvest time; although this only defines the season-starting activity. Once the actual harvest is complete, attention must quickly be diverted to preparing for the next season; there is no time to tarry. It is expected in this season that your seed has ripened and the cycle of growth is complete.

Because the focus is heavily dominated by reaping activity, the other affairs of life sometimes go *on pause*. During the pause, we lower our guard, take our focus off the calendar and celebrate. This uncovers the hidden danger of the fall season. Getting too comfortable, sets the stage for a quicker fall or delay when the unpredictable cold returns. Therefore, the lesson is to enjoy the harvest, never underestimate season change and always have your field and farming resources nearby and ready for use.

In a practical sense, as it relates to parenting - because the seasons don't necessarily represent a specific period of time, we must be careful not to become too literal and expect or force harvest when it's not appropriate. It is important to evaluate the situation, understand your child's positioning (or yours for that matter) and decide what's best from there.

When we don't understand the concept of seasons in this manner - especially in unfavorable seasons—we may start to believe that our seasons aren't changing and never will. In this headspace, we may stop cultivating, stop planting, stop nourishing, stop trusting, stop dreaming, stop taking risks, and at times stop living. This is what ultimately leads to defeat, crop failure and famine. This topic will be covered in *Chapter 12: The Famine*.

What should be clear is that life happens in seasons, and these seasons change, sometimes rapidly, and at times in a recurring fashion. The objective is to always be aware of what season we are in so that we can act accordingly. Each season plays a role in the overall plan and there is always a lesson to both teach and learn.

PART FOUR:
Advanced Farming

As with farming, extreme or uncommon circumstances arise and another level of knowledge, skill and understanding is required. What worked in a traditional sense of things may not for situations that have added complexity or dissimilar characteristics from the norm.

In the chapters following, a few Advanced Farming situations will be presented in brief to give some insight and perspective on how to view and approach the situation, if relevant. Each of these topics, though complex in nature, further validate the importance of following the farming process as written in *Part Three: The Field Guide To Parenting*. Completely disregarding or even partially executing the various steps of the seed preparation, planting, nourishing and harvesting process can lead to extreme outcomes.

Provided you find yourself in the middle or beginning phases of any of these advanced topics, be first reminded that there is hope. Along with this hope comes a responsibility to own the failure and make immediate restitution – which in most cases ultimately becomes the stalled place for change. Thus, as you recognize your situation to be in an advanced farming state, evaluate the cost of your penitence and/or labor to resolve against the expense of potentially losing your seed and the great generation to follow.

The choice should be easy to make, but many people have difficulty owning the outcomes of their decisions and allow "what is" excuses and stubbornness to cloud "what could be". Complete exposure, transparency and vulnerability unfortunately bring about fear in some people. Sadly, many don't realize that this is actually the space where freedom, peace and prosperity live.

CHAPTER 10
Bad Seed

According to The Georgia Crop Improvement Association, "Growers tend to blame bad seed, but even good seed won't sprout in bad conditions."[13] Based on this quote, one could argue that there really is no such thing as a bad seed and that all seeds originate equal and 'good'. In saying this, there are parents who think that their child was 'just born bad' and that there is no hope in rejuvenating positivity, goodness and purpose in their child. This mindset and belief is furthest from the truth.

> *"A healthy tree cannot bear bad fruit, nor can a diseased tree bear good fruit."*
> *Matthew 7:18*

This scriptural verse further confirms that it is not the seed that *own's its own* bad, but it is instead the circumstances and reflection of its maker that determines its state of being. Everything that a seed is and endures, and what the seed becomes is a direct reflection of the tree – otherwise known as *you*.

> *And he told them many things in parables, saying: "A sower went out to sow. And as he sowed, some seeds fell along the path, and the birds came and devoured them. Other seeds fell on rocky ground, where they did not have much soil, and immediately they sprang up, since they had no depth of soil, but when the sun rose they were scorched. And since they had no root, they withered*

---

[13] Clint Thompson, UGA CAES, "Cool Soils, Not Poor Seed Quality, Likely The Cause Of Poor Peanut Stands", accessed March 28, 2018. http://www.georgiacrop.com/cool-soils-not-poor-seed-quality-likely-the-cause-of-poor-peanut-stands

away. Other seeds fell among thorns, and the thorns grew up and choked them. Other seeds fell on good soil and produced grain, some a hundredfold, some sixty, some thirty.
Matthew 13:3-9

Again, scripture validates there is no such thing as bad seed, but instead good seed that was uncultivated and not inspired for greatness.

So, if you are feeling hopeless and defeated, and have exhausted efforts to help your child improve his behavior and get on the road to greatness, you are a prime candidate for a rebirthing experience. Only by God's grace, our reverence, faith-filled and sin-less life can we ultimately produce good seed. The truth is achieving seeds of greatness, cannot happen based on our mere belief systems; a relationship with God is required.

"since you have been born again, not of perishable seed but of imperishable, through the living and abiding word of God;"
1 Peter 1:23

CHAPTER 11
Contemporary Mixed Cropping

Mixed cropping, also known as polyculture, inter-cropping, or co-cultivation, is a type of agriculture that involves planting two or more plants simultaneously in the same field allowing them to grow together.[14] The logic behind this farming technique is that planting multiple crops at the same time minimizes space constraints, especially in situations where crops harvest in different seasons. Other benefits to planting crops simultaneously include improved weeds, insect and field management, soil protection, and a general increase in productivity.

While these benefits appear to bring extreme value and advantage, recognizing that mixed farming systems require multiple activities to run at the same time demonstrates the difficulty in controlling, monitoring and maintaining the farm. Additionally, there are times when one activity may hinder another – which provides little to no benefit at the end of the day.

At first read, mixed cropping from a parenting perspective could represent a twin or multiple birth with your mate. Though true and sharing the same benefits and considerations as a farming plan where multiple seeds were planted - modern day relationships have changed the state of this agricultural process and created a "mixed crop" parenting platform where children are birthed from multiple relationships. Often, at the same time.

Co-parenting with multiple mates and giving equal and fair time to each child presents a high degree of complexity and challenge; which

---
[14] "Mixed Cropping: History of the Ancient Farming Technique", accessed May 2, 2018. https://www.thoughtco.com/mixed-cropping-history-171201

conceivably could become the root cause for a failed harvest.

Each seed, as we have discussed in *Part Three: The Field Guide To Parenting* requires an individual amount of dedication. Each child should receive adequate and equal engagement and inspiration. Which, in essence supports the idea of having multiple seeds. Thus, the concern is not having multiple children with a single mate (on a single field), but birthing multiple children as a result of random, unplanned and/or ubiquitous seed plantings.

Unlike a singular family unit with multiple children, where there are consistent preparations, plans, farming practices and decisions, today's mixed cropping structure is flawed and does not lend itself to long-term greatness for anyone.

So again, not following the farming process covered in this book for each individual child has lasting effects and consequences. With the lack of focus and planning being huge contributors, mixed cropping is simply not recommended as a method of cultivating a single seed nor building a generation of greatness.

CHAPTER 12
The Famine

Brought on by a variety of factors, crop failure being one, a scarcity of food could become an escalated state for a community or population. This lack or shortage is formally called a famine and along with it comes malnutrition, starvation and an increased possibility of death. History tells us that famine has been experienced by every inhabited continent in the world, with some areas being more impacted than others.

Due to changing agricultural conditions and variations in weather, crops have been more susceptible for failure in some parts of the world. To impact this problem, other countries have stepped in to provide assistance and nourishment, as well as farming processes being adopted that have improved the production of sustainable crops.

From a practical or parenting perspective, famine can also be a realistic fate for some families or communities. When any seed ceases to be productive and lives in a state of "dead", there lies an active famine. When a community stops thriving and only survives from the lifeline of receiving, there lies an active famine. Where there is no growth, there is decline. Where there is no life or inspiration, there is death. Where there is no change and repentance, there will be no transformation or healing.

> *"If I shut up the heavens so that there is no rain, or if I command the locust to devour the land, or if I send pestilence among My people, and My people who are called by My name humble themselves and pray and seek My face and turn from their wicked ways, then I will hear from heaven, will forgive their sin and will heal their land. "Now My eyes will be open and My ears attentive to the prayer offered in this place....*
> 2 Chronicles 7:13-15

In this verse, there is evidently a punishment in action; one that impacts the growth and possibility of harvest (ie. no rain, demolished land, dying population). The goodness of God however, is that He offers a way to improve the situation and bring relief, healing and prosperity back to a broken, impoverished and unfruitful land.

As stated, there are three such requests – humbling oneself, pray and seeking God's face, and turning away from sin. Interestingly, none of these requests give order to *how to fix the seed or land*, but yet the requirement is of the *seed bearer or land owner*. Even in a moment of famine and extreme loss, there is a turn-around possible and affirmed. We have a recourse available to reverse the current situation and end the desolate state of our crops.

The question isn't *what was wrong with the harvest causing it to fail;* the question is *what was my role in the failure of the harvest.*

- How many more children do I have to witness committing a crime or offense before I actively impact the problem?
- How many more people have to be hurt from the hurt of another before I do something different?
- How dedicated am I to my seed and the seeds to come?
- How bad do I want to see positive change?
- How much am I willing to sacrifice to achieve this positive change?

And so, answering these questions affirmatively and embodying action revolutionizes *the change* – the once unthinkable, thought-impossible change. Thereby building an **Inspired|Legacy**.

APPENDIX

Top 25 Crimes, Offenses and Violations Referred to Youth Justice Diversion Programs *http://www.globalyouthjustice.org/TOP_25_CRIMES.html*

#1
Theft/Larceny
Typical Cases
Shoplifting, Stealing a Bicycle, Stealing from Backpacks and Lockers,

#2
Vandalism
Typical Cases
Tagging and Graffiti, Drawing on Public Restroom Walls, Keying a Car and Cutting, Auto Tires

#3
Alcohol Offenses
Typical Cases
Underage Purchase or Possession, Underage Consumption of Alcohol, Providing Alcohol to Underage Persons, Possessing an Open Container in Public/Car

#4
Disorderly Conduct
Typical Cases
Fighting in a Public Place, Cursing at a Teacher, Flashing, Mooning and Indecent, Exposure

#5
Simple Assault or Battery
Typical Cases
Bullying when it Amounts to Assault, Child/Parent Physical Disagreements, Shoving or Pushing a Person

#6
Possession of Marijuana
Typical Cases
Possessing Small Amounts of Marijuana, Smoking Marijuana in a Public Place,

#7
Tobacco Offenses
Typical Cases
Illegally Purchasing Tobacco, Chewing or Smoking Tobacco at School, Providing or Enabling Youth to Use Tobacco

#8
Curfew Violations

Typical Cases
Sneaking Out of Home After Curfew, Walking Home After Curfew, Violating a Park Curfew

#9
School Disciplinary Offense
Typical Cases
Disrupting Class, Food Fights and Cheating, Violating the Dress Code

#10
Traffic Violations
Typical Cases
Speeding or Failing to Yield, Not Wearing a Seat Belt, Riding in the Back of a Pickup Truck

#11
Truancy
Typical Cases
Cutting Class, Having Excessive Tardies, Violating Court Order to Attend School

#12
Criminal Trespass
Typical Cases
Entering a Vacant Building, Entering Land or a Dwelling Without Permission, Returning to a Store After Being Banned

#13
Mischief/Criminal Nuisance
Typical Cases
Damaging a Mailbox, Egging or Toilet-papering a House, Picking Flowers in a Restricted or Private Area

#14
Possession of Drug Paraphernalia
Typical Cases
Having a Pipe in Pocket with Resin, Using Drug Paraphernalia to Use a Controlled Substance, Possessing Drug Paraphernalia to Grow Marijuana

#15
Harassment
Typical Cases
Bullying, Making Telephone Calls Without Good Reason, Insulting or Taunting Another Person to Provoke a Disorderly Response

#16
Fraud
Typical Cases
Writing Bad Checks, Impersonating Another Person, Committing Fraud Via E-Mail

#17
Burglary
Typical Cases
Enter Friends or Relatives Homes to Steal Something, Entering a School Building to Steal Something, Entering a Home/School and Causing Damage

#18
False Reporting
Typical Cases
Pulling a Fire Alarm, Calling in False 911 Calls, Calling in a Bomb Threat

#19
Loitering
Typical Cases
Hanging Out in a Group in Front of a Building, Smoking in Groups on the Street Corner, Being in a Park or Store After Closing

#20
Possession of Stolen Property
Typical Cases
Having a Bicycle you know is Stolen, Receiving Stolen Goods from a Friend, Being in the Company of Someone Who is Stealing

#21
Possession of a Weapon
Typical Cases
Unlawfully Possessing Pepper Spray, Possessing a BB or Pellet Gun While Underage, Carrying Weapons like Metal Knuckles or Nunchucks

#22
Reckless Endangerment
Typical Cases
Throwing Snowballs at Cars, Hanging on to a Moving Car, Speeding Out of a Parking Lot

#23
Resisting an Officer without Violence
Typical Cases
Lying to a Police Officer, including one's Age, Running Away from Law Enforcement, Refusing

to Move When, Ordered by an Officer

#24
Runaways
Typical Cases
Running Away from a Noncustodial Parents House, Going to another City/State when Forbidden by a Parent, Staying at a Friend or Families House without Parent Permission

#25
Unauthorized Use of a Motor Vehicle
Typical Cases
Driving Without a License, Unlawfully Using All-Terrain Vehicles (ATV's), Taking Parents or Friends Car without Permission

The Legend Exercise (reference pages 33-38)

Answer	Agricultural Term	Scenario – Physical Interpretation
	Land / Soil	A. My children, collectively
	Field	B. I made every effort to surround myself with positive influences, learn as much as possible about self-care and save money before I had my first child.
	Cultivate	C. My spouse has such strong values and those values are being passed down to our children.
	Sow	D. We purposely chose the community where we live based on the surrounding atmosphere, general spirit of the neighborhood and progressiveness of the people around us.
	Seed	E. It is a wonder and joyful moment to see my baby growing in my womb.
	Reap / Harvest	F. My child
	Fruit	G. I'm always watchful of the company my children keep; making sure that they are not bad influences or leading them astray.
	Crop	H. I'm careful about what I say to my son because I want to make sure that what he hears from me becomes a part of who he is and manifests into something positive and great when he becomes an adult.
	Germination	I. Now as adults, my children are very loving and kind; which reflects everything they were taught.
	Weeds	J. My children have all matured to be strong, loving and productive people, who give back graciously to their community.

The Legend Exercise **Answers**

Answer	Agricultural Term	Scenario – Physical Interpretation
D	Land / Soil	A. My children, collectively
C	Field	B. I made every effort to surround myself with positive influences, learn as much as possible about self-care and save money before I had my first child.
B	Cultivate	C. My spouse has such strong values and those values are being passed down to our children.
H	Sow	D. We purposely chose the community where we live based on the surrounding atmosphere, general spirit of the neighborhood and progressiveness of the people around us.
F	Seed	E. It is a wonder and joyful moment to see my baby growing in my womb.
I	Reap / Harvest	F. My child
J	Fruit	G. I'm always watchful of the company my children keep; making sure that they are not bad influences or leading them astray.
A	Crop	H. I'm careful about what I say to my son because I want to make sure that what he hears from me becomes a part of who he is and manifests into something positive and great when he becomes an adult.
E	Germination	I. Now as adults, my children are very loving and kind; which reflects everything they were taught.
G	Weeds	J. My children have all matured to be strong, loving and productive people, who give back graciously to their community.

Cultivation Audit (reference pages 61-66)

The statements below in the **Self** section should be answered **from your perspective**, about YOU, as things are TODAY. You will respond using a scale of 0-5 for the selected response. A sample entry is shown, S0.

0=No opinion, 1=Totally Agree, 2=Moderately Agree, 3=Neutral, 4=Moderately Disagree, 5=Totally Disagree

		Totally Agree	Moderately Agree	Neutral	Moderately Disagree	Totally Disagree	No Opinion / NA
SELF							
S0	I plan to respond to this Self-Assessment honestly.					5	
S1	I have room in my life to take on the demands of parenting.						
S2	I have a solid relationship with my mate.						
S3	I have achieved balance with my career to soon take on the full responsibility of parenting.						
S4	I am comfortable with how much I've achieved toward my personal aspirations and current life goals.						
S5	My spiritual foundation is solid and I have a stable grasp on my purpose, gifts and talents.						
S6	I have achieved balance with family/friends and defined a fair expectation on how much time I can commit to them once becoming a parent.						
S7	I am emotionally ready to responsible for a child.						
S8	I have named and responded to my Indirect Affects as mentioned in Chapter 2.						
S9	I am confident in my selection process for a mate.						
S10	I have analyzed and cultivated appropriately.						
S11	I am a flexible, open-minded person with a willingness to learn and adapt to things I've never done before or not done well.						
	SELF SECTION TOTAL						

The statements in the **Mate** section should be answered from **your perspective**, about YOUR MATE, as things are TODAY. You will respond using a scale of 0-5 for the selected response. A sample entry is shown, M0.

0=No opinion, **1**=Totally Agree, **2**=Moderately Agree, **3**=Neutral, **4**=Moderately Disagree, **5**=Totally Disagree

		Totally Agree	Moderately Agree	Neutral	Moderately Disagree	Totally Disagree	No Opinion / NA
MATE							
M0	*I plan to respond to this Self-Assessment honestly.*		4				
M1	I know my mate well.						
M2	It is evident that my mate has produced good fruit relative to their own children and/or children they have influence over.						
M3	It is evident that my mate has produced good fruit relative to their personal affairs.						
M4	It is evident that my mate has produced good fruit relative to their professional affairs.						
M5	It is evident that my mate has a solid spiritual foundation and healthy fear and reverence for God.						
M6	It is evident that my mate is able to handle stressful or unpredictable situations well because of their spiritual foundation.						
M7	My mate lives in a state of positivity and hopefulness because of their spiritual foundation.						
M8	My mate lives out unconditional love and is able to love thru the tough times.						
M9	My mate has demonstrated that he/she can love someone that has wronged them.						
M10	My mate is able to show love, as well as speak it.						
M11	My mate does not keep record or rehash wrong doings.						

M12	My mate has demonstrated their ability to forgive and seek to understand, rather than seek to be right.	
M13	We have committed ourselves to parenting a child by all means necessary.	
M14	My mate and I have a recipe for success and happiness that is based on knowing our purpose, executing with our gifts and talents, and ultimately surviving off what we give to others - in hopes of improving their lives.	
M15	My mate and I stand firm on all decisions we've made to date.	
	MATE SECTION TOTAL	
	CULTIVATION AUDIT TOTAL	

Record your results below.

	Green		Yellow		Red	
	Low	High	Low	High	Low	High
Self	0	11	12	33	34	55
Mate	0	15	16	45	46	75
Total	0	26	27	78	79	130

Farming Inspiration Resources

Acquaah, G. 2002. "Land Preparation and Farm Energy" pp. 318–38 in *Principles of Crop Production, Theories, Techniques and Technology*. Prentice Hall, Upper Saddle River, NJ.

Acquaah, G. 2002. "Soil and Land" pp. 165–210 in *Principles of Crop Production, Theories, Techniques and Technology*. Prentice Hall, Upper Saddle River, NJ.

Acquaah, G. 2002. "Plants and Soil Water" pp. 211–39 in *Principles of Crop Production, Theories, Techniques and Technology*. Prentice Hall, Upper Saddle River, NJ.

"Chapter VI: Land Preparation, Planting Operation and Fertilization Requirements, by P. Klein and A. Zaid Date. http://www.fao.org/docrep/006/Y4360E/y4360e0a.htm

"Four Seasons of Farming", by Haleyv11, Western Illinois University School of Agriculture. https://wiuag.wordpress.com/2016/10/24/four-seasons-of-farming

"Harvesting", Encyclopedia of Food and Culture. https://www.encyclopedia.com/sports-and-everyday-life/food-and-drink/food-and-cooking/harvesting

"Mixed Cropping History of the Ancient Farming Technique", by K. Kris Hirst, Updated October 23, 2017. https://www.thoughtco.com/mixed-cropping-history-171201

"Post-planting cultivation in a conservation plan", Iowa State University Extension and Outreach, Integrated Crop Management. https://crops.extension.iastate.edu/post-planting-cultivation-conservation-plan

"Ten worst famines of the 20th century". Sydney Morning Herald. 15 August 2011. Archived from the original on 3 July 2014.

Wikipedia, https://en.wikipedia.org/wiki/Farm, https://en.wikipedia.org/wiki/Growing_season

More than a book title, **INSPIRED|LEGACY** *is a movement;* ushering **The GREAT Revolution**.

The Motto
Inspire. Dream. Be™

The Mission
To stir up the silence and *ignite a spark* in the parent-child relationship that *inspires a vision* and *creates a greater state of being*.

The Why
The Why is enhanced by The Who. *Our children* are the future and there is a critical need to ensure the life and experience of tomorrow has promise. Thus, inspiring generational greatness becomes the every-day, every-moment mission.

www.ingramcontent.com/pod-product-compliance
Lightning Source LLC
Chambersburg PA
CBHW050909160426
43194CB00011B/2339